COSTUMES AND SETTINGS FOR HISTORICAL PLAYS

Volume 5
The Nineteenth Century

COSTUMES AND SETTINGS FOR HISTORICAL PLAYS

JACK CASSIN-SCOTT

Volume 5
The Nineteenth Century

B T Batsford Limited London

© Jack Cassin-Scott 1980
First published 1980
ISBN 0 7134 1710 2

Printed in Great Britain by
The Anchor Press Limited
Tiptree, Essex
for the publishers
B T Batsford Limited
4 Fitzhardinge Street
London W1H 0AH

CONTENTS

INTRODUCTION

This book, the fifth volume in the series *Costumes and Settings for Historical Plays*, attempts to show some of the essential features of historical costume and stage settings between the years of 1815 to 1900. The characteristic features of this period have been recorded by plays and pictorial works which are our main source of study, and which are, by and large, beyond controversy. They provide us with a foundation on which the historical stage designer may safely build and give us enough material to show how an era of history reflects itself in theatre design.

To write the complete history of theatre arts or of costume design, even just for this period alone, would require more than this modest volume. Nonetheless to define a period of history through the medium of the theatre, is, within certain limits, feasible, although it is important to bear in mind that the structure of stage design must remain in a controversial state as long as it is based on vague abstractions or generalities. What is attempted in this volume is to foster an individualistic attitude and to avoid empty or biased generalizations.

The theatre of the nineteenth century was noted for its heavy scenic displays. The empty stage of the Elizabethan theatre, depending largely on the imagination of the spectator, proved its own inadequacy. The eloquent description of a scene which did not exist was far from satisfactory, except when scenic effects were not available, but such eloquence could not and cannot achieve the same effectiveness as a well designed stage setting. There is today a tendency to present a barren empty stage as the focal background to the play. This may save money, but unless it conveys something to the audience, and fairly quickly, the entertainment value, which must be the main object of the play, is lost. In the majority of historical plays the six main ingredients must always be present: the dramatist, producer, scenic

In the year 1899, women's clothes were modelled on the princess-line style. The waist is close-fitting and a white silk pelisse boa hangs round the neck. A toque of tulle is decorated with bird-of-paradise feathers. The gentleman is wearing the double-breasted frock overcoat

The lady of 1897 is wearing the bolero jacket with leg-o-mutton shoulder sleeves. The sportsman has a Norfolk jacket suit with the three-quarter length cape

Short hair with thin beard style, 1871

Full beard and short hairstyle 1892

designer, actor, costume designer and lighting expert. All their separate arts are fused together in the creation of a play.

Research is a necessary preliminary to a methodical approach towards the achievement of historical accuracy and the importance of this cannot be over-stressed. The aim of the historical aspect is to interpret individual objects, not primarily or necessarily to make beautiful objects, but to produce believeable equivalents for the historical stage play.

Scenic designing is not an easy task and full of pitfalls, but the true designer willingly tolerates what others cannot. Today the area controlled by the designer of stage settings has a wealth of modern materials at its disposal. Through the continued showing of historical plays the theatre of today maintains the links between the ancient and the modern worlds. It is the stage designer who through the skill he exercises must understand the subtle and gradual changes of fashion throughout any given period in history and who must interpret them for the audience.

Theatre is in itself a curious phenomenon since it unites a group of people whose purpose is to create an artificial myth in a world of harsh realities. The position of the designer within this group is of fundamental importance for any understanding of an historical stage play. It is he who before any word of dialogue is uttered, must first convey the time and place of the historic piece through the stage setting, costumes and properties. Nonetheless the producer does have the final say and this either directly or indirectly has some influence on the designer.

There is an abundance of illustrative material available showing the costumes and architectural designs of the period described in this volume. In the latter years photography has taken over from artists' impressions and this has provided recorded evidence in perhaps greater detail than ever before. The illustrations in this book have greatly used these sources and it is the author's hope that they show the costumes as they were worn throughout the period, with some authenticity. The foundation formula, on which most of these costumes are based is not however simplified in the illustrations as it is these original representations which are the designer's main works of reference for the characteristics and features of the period.

An exaggeration of line and colour must always be part of a designer's 'make-up', without which the impact of a

There was great poverty in the Victorian era and often the clothes of the people were ragged and ill-fitting. This couple in the year 1882 shows a woman in a market seller's clothing with an apron. The ragged urchin has closely cropped hair and a bedraggled hand-me-down suit

character and a costume could be lost in the background. There is one basic theme, a theme illustrated again and again throughout this series and it is as important today as it has ever been; that is, the whole effect must be 'larger than life'.

It is often a simplification to regard stage properties as a minor part of the set design and the designer must beware of this since it could be likened to a wedding cake without the decoration — an impossible thought! A designer who cannot make his or her own stage properties or hasn't a good property master by his side is facing a task with one hand tied behind his back. Such is the importance of stage properties as stage dressing and for atmospheric authenticity. It is of equal importance to scenic design, whose existence and function, both in theory and practice is inseparably bound up with stage properties.

There is such a wealth of material from which historical plays (or costume plays) can be produced in this period, from straight plays to the musical comedies which abounded in the theatre of the last century. The choice is endless, for many of the great dramatists of both the nineteenth and twentieth centuries wrote plays in the costume and dressing of our selected era.

Lighting has now become a vital part of stage setting; the subtle blending of colours can create untold moods and atmospheres far beyond the scope of the artist's brush. Any production, no matter how small, cannot create the 'living picture' without a minimum of lighting equipment. Although lighting can, in very exceptional cases, be used alone on a barren stage with great effect, its true function is its fusing with the other skills and arts of the theatre. A study of the science of lighting should be included in every young designer's plan of theatre arts, so that it is not merely illumination, but an important part of the whole stage setting. Light, just like the action of a play, is a moving, vibrant part of the stage 'picture'.

The abundance of reference material for the nineteenth century ranging from engravings to photographs has been used as a basis for the line drawings to show the salient points of costume and stage settings. Plays and musical shows have been listed not merely to offer a selection but to stimulate the reader into putting on a costume spectacular. The Music Hall, Musical Comedy and the English Pantomime were very much a part of this era, and to reproduce them now is both a challenge and an exercise in the world of theatrical entertainment.

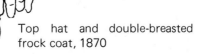

Top hat and double-breasted frock coat, 1870

THE COSTUME

Small ragged boy selling news-papers, 1890s

Costume can often be the highlight or the semi-disaster of the historical play. When creating stage costume it must be remembered that it is an important and integral part of the stage design, a part that must blend and harmonize with all the other component arts which make the historical play. The form and silhouette should easily identify to the audience the period piece being enacted, never clashing with the authentic background, yet offering sufficient contrast to stand out.

Only when the costume designer has firmly established in his own mind the precise period of time covered by the play and the social standing of the individuals in the various roles can he set about the difficult and time-consuming job of research.

As his sources the designer must consult museums, picture galleries, libraries specializing in old photographs, theatre journals, magazines and as many books as possible. Then the costume designer moves to the next phase which is to ask the producer for his comments and approval and finally the actor or actress who is to be costumed.

Although imaginative garments are to be recommended, historical dress must of necessity primarily evoke the period of the play being enacted. On the other hand it should not be the exact replica of an antique costume but rather it should outline its general features. The form, silhouette and the appropriate choice of colour are the prime essentials.

Another important part of costume design is always to remember that the design is to fit an individual and not a dummy. In most cases the individual is more important than the costume, so the garment must be subordinate to the person. If the costume fails to help convey the character that the actor is attempting to portray then it is not a good costume design, or if it attracts more attention at the expense of the actor it has again failed.

Lady in a promenade dress of 1883 in the polonaise style, with a tight coat bodice buttoned down the centre front with laced lapels, side panniers puffed out in the pompadours fashion. Fashionable men in the same period wore the knee-length frock-coat with the single-breasted waistcoat of a different colour cut square at the base

Decoration is very important in costume design, but again it must not be the centre of attraction, taking the spectator's eye away from the main structure of the costume. The design is all-important, the decoration if overdone will be detrimental to that design; if it is used with discretion it will enhance the original form and design.

Planning a costume is not without its difficulties, a study of the anatomy of the human figure is an essential part of costume design and the possible action of the character must always be taken into consideration. Violent action such as dancing or gymnastics, leaping and duelling must be allowed for in the costume design. Therefore the movement of the part played by the actor must never be impeded by a bad design, and the costume designer must understand the role as much as the actor who must eventually play it. Only by this method can a designer really begin to understand and

◄ Travelling costume of 1894. The lady is wearing the French-style full to the ground sleeveless cloak with the Carrick multi-short ruched shoulder capes, and a straw hat with ribbon and flower decoration. The gentleman is in a fly-front Chesterfield

appreciate the importance of his or her part in the creative arts of the stage.

A knowledge of materials is of course a must in the art of costume design, as without it many of the effects would be lost and form and structure would be impossible to control. Fabric, like so many other things, varies in the way it handles. It can be stiff, soft, harsh or pliable, hang straight, or in folds. It can be cheap or costly. The cost factor is perhaps one of the greatest problems for the costume designer. It is always a dilemma when the production finances are discussed and a decision has to be made as to what proportion will be allocated to the costume or wardrobe department, and it is never enough. With such limitations imposed cheaper materials such as unbleached calico, cambric, hessian, must of necessity be used for most of the garments. Happily, with ingenuity such materials can be put to good use since the costume designer can incorporate these fabrics into his design so that they resemble the finest materials. With the help of the proper dyes and the deft use of stage lighting,

Women army camp-followers often dressed in the style of the regiment they were serving. The illustration shows two French so-called 'sultresses', often also called a vivandière or a cantinière. On the left a member of the Tirailleurs Indiens, on the right, Garde Pionnier

Fashions at the end of the nineteenth century. The bolero jacket with the large sleeve costume of 1896 and the day dress full to the ground with close-fitting sleeves

even the most discerning spectator can be led to believe that the costumes are manufactured from more expensive materials. Often, coarse-textured fabrics under good lighting conditions tend to give a warmer, livelier glow than smoother, expensive materials under the same lighting arrangements.

Colour schemes for costumes always present the designer with problems, so the art of dyeing becomes almost as important as the making of the costumes themselves. Both modern and old-fashioned methods are used: cold water dyes boiling and dipping, each method having its own par-

Close cut hair and full beard style 1895

ticular advantage. Dye is an easy commodity to purchase and is sold at all good haberdashery counters. When the colour has been chosen for the costume, it is essential that a small piece is subjected to the dye required and then placed under stage lighting conditions. If this is not carried out in a methodical and intelligent manner, the result could be disastrous, with the garment turning into hideous colours under the coloured lighting. Remember also that different materials react in different ways with the effect of dyes, so a certain amount of careful experimental try-outs must take place before deciding on both the materials and dyes to be used.

Learn something about dyes; how they are manufactured, what they contain as regards chemicals etc. Basically they fall into three categories: animal, vegetable and mineral. The last is more often used, especially with cottons and leather goods. Methods of applying dyes are fairly numerous, from bath dyeing (dipping and boiling), tie-dyeing, batik, spraying, stencilling and hand painting. The designer who has studied the art of dyeing will be able to blend the colour and the costumes into the overall picture of the stage setting. With the added aid of analine dye (extensively used also by scenic artists) colours available can be quite strong, almost garish as opposed to the more pastel shades of the other dyes. A word of advice here: colour should be experimented with and only by trial and error will ultimate success be assured.

Looking at the nineteenth century it must appear to be a somewhat confusing one to the young costume designer since the dates and names of the various fashions present some difficulty. First is the Restoration (of the French King Louis XVIII) 1815 to 1820; the Biedermeier Style and the Romantic Era 1820 to 1840; Early Victorian or Second Rococo or the Crinoline Style 1840 to 1870; the Victorian Era or the Bustle Style 1870 to 1890, and finally the End of the Century 1890 to 1900. Although one will meet these names throughout the lengthy research which must take place it will be more expedient and less time-consuming to place them (without confusing the issue further) under the headings of Regency (1810-20); Romantic Period (1820-37); Early Victorian Period (1837-57); Mid-Victorian Period (1857-77), and Late Victorian Period (1877-1900). The gradual changes can then be more easily dated.

Lady in a day dress with a bodice, closed round the neck with a low standing collar. The full skirt is slightly trained at the back. The gentleman is in the single-breasted frock coat with the large neck cloth

Within the Regency period came the restoration of the French royal family after the defeat and exile of Napoleon when the Treaty of Paris once again gave the Bourbons their place on the French throne.

In *women's fashion* the female figure which had been allowed to be natural under the high-waisted transparent muslin dresses which had been in vogue was once more

Country style gingham dress with large bonnet, 1860

being subjected to artificial corsetry. By the beginning of the Romantic era (1820) the waistline was lowered and the skirts took on a greater fullness. The cylinder shape with the narrow shoulders and wide hemline of the skirt gradually changed to become wider at the shoulders with the addition of the large leg-o-mutton type sleeves, and the shortened skirt of almost equal width. The waistline was constricted to its smallest possible dimension. Fashion still favoured the Greek influence in women's modes along with the fifteenth- and sixteenth-century frilled collars and the puff sleeves revival. The military styles of the Napoleonic era still persisted in the popular female riding costumes of the day.

The engravings and caricatures of the nineteenth century are well worth studying and their use will help enormously in theatre costume design by adding that little touch of extreme high fashion which was so prevalent and popular in the fashionable world of that time. The young costume designer must also realise that in the more remote countryside, fashions changed slowly, therefore a mixture of old and new styles is quite acceptable when designing a play of this period, and earlier styles should be studied. Volume 4 of this series outlines these costumes.

The late Romantic period ushered in a more elegant style with the dresses attaining a bell shape which continued in fashion with slight modifications over the next two decades. Hairstyles, too, slowly became more elegant with a centre parting and side curls.

The early Victorian period saw the bell-shaped silhouette, a small bell-shape skirt in soft light materials with the long pointed narrow bodice being adopted by all fashionable people. By the early mid-Victorian era with the invention of the sewing machine came the profusion of wider and wider skirts made with heavier and heavier materials and much ornamental trimming. At this point when the overwhelming mass of the thick material and decoration was becoming almost unbearable to wear the lightweight wire hoop came into fashion. This contraption (as such it was) took the weight and the balance of these enormous skirts, resulting in a further widening of the skirt and nether garments. The outerwear became more capacious to allow for the covering of the lower half of the figure. Hairstyles remained small with centre partings with side curls covering the ears. A poke bonnet style headwear usually covered this simple hairstyle.

Such are the vagaries of fashion that by the late sixties the crinoline in a transitional stage was flattened in the front and the mass of skirt material was pulled up and pushed behind. The bustle silhouette was upon the fashionable scene supported by 'crinolette' wire frames protruding at the back only.

The Late Victorian era saw the tailor-made dresses of silk and taffeta and the bustle protruding further out at the back. But by the late 1880s the bustle began to shrink in size and by 1890 had disappeared almost entirely. The end of the century saw blouses, hip-length jackets and long trailing skirts and the popular 'Gibson Girl' styles became all the rage. Sportive clothes for cycling and tennis and other activities were all very popular.

From the Regency times the male fashion began to take on a more formal style, the breeches and stockings of the previous era were waning in popularity. Coming into fashion was the long to the ankle trouser (pantaloons) fashion. These, like the waistcoats, were often in brighter colours than the more sombre-coloured jacket. The silhouette was, however, somewhat feminine in appearance with deeply waisted coats and broad hiplines.

The Romantic era saw very little change in men's clothes; the frock coat was straight-fitting to the knee, although cut-away coats were still in vogue. The trousers were full at the waist, tapering slightly to the ankle and secured by a strap under the instep, 'cossack' style. Adopted at this time was the shiny glossy silk top hat, to replace the early beaver-type hat. These hats were fairly tall and slender with narrow brims.

In early Victorian times men's clothes, in general, became more rational and sombre in appearance with a straight-fitting frock coat with wide baggy (often plaid) trousers hanging in unseemly folds at the ankles. The older styles of the forties however were still worn, adding a touch of elegance in contrast to the newer, looser and obviously more comfortable styles entering the male fashionable world.

A study of the cutting patterns for males of this period would prove most useful to the young costume designer. There are some very interesting books available on this subject. The Late Victorian period saw the male costume sombre in colour but with elegant styling and cut. More informal wear like the Norfolk jacket became very much the everyday wear of most classes of society.

Cut of the 1899 style frock coat

Bolero jacket costume in the large sleeve style, 1895

The general colours which were popular are mentioned in the main body of the text on costume along with the description of the various styles worn by both male and female to improve their outward appearance.

Regency 1810-1820

The economical and political climate of Europe underwent great changes especially after the defeat and exile of Napoleon in 1815. The aftermath of war had left Europe greatly

Lady in the Spencer and pelerine fashion of 1825 with a bonnet and fringed parasol. The male figure is after Alfred D'Orsay, 'the last of the dandies', wearing the wide lapel mode of 1828

Male and female fashions of the early 1820s. Pantaloons were now the most fashionable dress for men and the popular redingote dress for women

disillusioned and the industrial revolution began to change the whole social structure. The middle classes, who had begun to influence fashion in the mid-eighteenth century now took it over almost entirely with their more powerful, wealthier numbers. Moral liberalism and materialistic attitudes ran side by side and these, coupled with the new technical innovations made many far-reaching changes.

The developing Americas now rivalled India in cotton production, forcing down the prices in the textile industries, producing cheaper materials for use in the growing European costume market. This greatly affected costume at all levels of society and the stage costume designer can now detect the changes which lay ahead. The waistlines of the women's costumes went back to their natural position, skirts although shorter, became wider and more flared. The bodice, which had been narrower during the Empire period, now became larger. Sleeves became large, increasing to the leg-o-mutton vogue.

The outstanding lasting outcome of this period as far as clothes are concerned was the Anglomania which swept over Paris. France adopted the male English tailoring, whilst England accepted the French female fashions. This mutual acceptance remains in force to this day.

The Regency and Restoration periods were indeed the hey-day of the English dandy. Along with the fastidious taste in dress came the gestures, polite impertinence, sarcasm and elegance which clung to these eccentric young men throughout. Today these fantastic characters are the ideal models for this period, they are figures that will never be seen again except through the eyes of the costume designers of historical plays. The perfect figure of the period was found in the Englishman, Beau Brummell (1778-1840), whose elegance and 'dandified' appearance swept Europe and made the term 'English' fashionable.

Although *trousers* (pantaloons) were introduced again during this period the knee-breeches were worn at court and all very formal occasions. The dandies however affected the trouser styles which came very high almost to the armpits and were secured in place by broad tapes which passed over the shoulders and fastened to the trousers by buttons, known as braces. Towards the end of the period trousers known as Peterham had striped flounces at the bottom.

After the Battle of Waterloo in 1815, there were a variety

The high-waisted pelisse dress with the broad padded hem line and bustle pad at the back was worn in 1824, although, by 1825, the waistline moved down and this dress was worn with a pelerine

23

The voluminous caped cloak and top hat fashion for men was popular for the winter of 1823. Ruffs and flounces were à la mode for ladies of this year

24

The ladies are dressed in the ball costumes of the 1880s, with the cuirass (plastron) bodice. The Russian officer in the foreground is in the colourful 1830 uniform of the Pavlowsky Grenadier Guards. The grenadier cap had a brass front

The fashions over the nineteenth century are depicted here, the lady on the left is in the mode of 1815. The gentleman is dressed in the costume of 1848 and the centre lady is in the fashion of 1879

of *boots* with such names as Blücher and Wellington, and those with the pointed front were called Hessian boots. Shoes with buckles were still worn with knee-breeches and for all ceremonial occasions.

The double-breasted tail coat with a low waistline and curving away tails over the hips followed a silhouette of a feminine nature with the narrow waist and wide hips. This form was achieved either by good tailoring, with the bodice cut and tapered to a close-fitting waist and the tails, made in separate pieces from the bodice, being flared and pleated over the hips for fullness, or by the waist being drawn in by a corset or a tightly laced waistcoat.

The next unusual aspect of the male attire, especially where the dandies were concerned, was the *neckwear*. This became the most important item of the male costume and there were some 32 methods in which a cravat could be tied. The costume designer would be well advised to study the creative art of neckwear to give the costume the correct style and feeling of the period.

Regardless of the passage of time the one thing which has remained with us from the period of the dandies is the *frock coat*. This continued in fashion throughout the nineteenth century into the twentieth century and remains with us in the form of a wedding frock coat, and an evening tail suit.

Women's Clothes This period was one of change or rather of modification, the pseudo-classical line remained with a greater emphasis on heavy ornamentation in trimmings. It was at this time that the reintroduction of the gored skirt and bodice took place; the skirt gored and gathered was extended from a short high waist (where it remained during this period), to a wide hemline which being only ankle length was heavily decorated with ornamental shapes to make it stand out. For day wear the skirt was untrained, but for evening it had a small, or demi-train. After about 1812 all dresses were untrained and the hemlines were profusely adorned with multiple flounces and frills, often with the material of the dress itself in the form of languettes, rolls and piped shapes. In addition to these trimmings were floral designs with artificial flowers, leaves of silk, vandyked borders and piped materials decorated with beads. The elegant 'Grecian bend' was achieved by inserting sausage-shaped rolls, secured under the waistline of the skirt. At

this time also the high-necked bodices came in again and the low-necked wide style was worn for evening, balls and ceremonial occasions with the dress being made with fewer folds. These dresses which were without folds and close-fitting, revealing the contours of the figure, were called robes en caleçon, and they were in fashion until the end of the Regency period. The costume designer must not confuse this style with the diaphanous flimsy dresses worn between 1800 and 1805.

Day dresses by 1817 were worn with a taffeta pelisse, with a standing collar and raised shoulder epaulettes. Round the neck was worn a fraise — a neck-ruff of pleated lace in two or three layers. By the end of the Regency period in 1820 the waistline was lowered to almost normal.

Outdoor garments Redingotes, also known under the Russian name of Witzschoura were a development of the earlier Greek style wrap-over tunic, sometimes taking the place of a cloak. By 1812 they were made with a broad turned-over collar with long, full, puffed gathered sleeves.

Popular during this period was the Spencer, a short jacket garment with long sleeves worn over the dress, and looking similar to the bodice of the high-necked dresses. A slight modification of both the Spencer and the bodice of the dress was the short puff shoulder sleeve which was worn over a fairly loose sleeve which was gathered at the wrist.

Although short sleeves were always present during this period, long sleeves were more popular and therefore more fashionable and they were in various styles. Often the longer sleeves were tubular or the small leg-o-mutton style.

A study of the court dresses of the time by the costume designer is made fairly easy by the many fine examples that can be seen in the museums. In the early part of the Regency period the hoop and the pannier were still worn in English court circles, although this old-fashioned style had long since disappeared in France under the revolution and among the fashionable people of England. English court dress was a somewhat strange mixture of styles and here the costume stage designer must use a great deal of discretion when planning these styles. The hoop and pannier, when worn with the newer high-waisted fashion produced a most unbalanced silhouette and lost the charm and beauty of both the old and the new vogues. By 1820, however, both the hoop and pannier contraptions were discarded and the

Two versions of the fashionable riding habits of different eras. The fashion of 1818 shown right is the Glengarry riding costume, richly ornamented with frogging and braiding and a high-stand collar with a full cravat. The lady on the left is wearing the habit of 1888 in the masculine style, a long hitched-up skirt and top hat

English court followed the style of the French with its elegant close-fitting dress with the long train.

Riding habits were very much a part of the feminine fashion world. They followed the male style and military style decorations prevailed. This military influence was very apparent with the showing of braiding and frogging in tailored habits. A fashionable design of 1817 was the Glengarry style, with its high-waisted, gored full skirt with side frogging. The masculine neck cloth high to the throat could be seen over the bodice which was frogged across the front. Over this was a tailless close-fitting jacket again frogged and braided with a high standing military collar and epaulettes. On the head was a tall crowned hat with feathers decorating the front. Heelless pumps with bows were worn on the feet. There were various styles of riding costume mainly in the masculine fashions both in cut and colour although there were some in brighter colours in greens and purples, very popular hues at this period. Wraps and shawls remained popular throughout the period, with added features such as long scarf-capes, lace fichus, pelisses with and without capes, and cloaks.

Jacket style bodice with full skirt, 1862

Headwear Hats of this period were indeed the true silhouette of the Regency era, and along with the coiffures, many of them increased in height. Some of these high crowned hats were covered in the same material as the dresses and trimmed with an edging of silk usually in the contrasting colour of the tippet (if worn). From 1816 the name of 'cornettes' was given to all indoor caps that were secured under the chin with ribbons, all others came under the title of 'mobs'. Both cornettes and mobs came in various sizes and shapes and materials as in the previous century. Outdoor hats and bonnets were constructed in such materials as silk, muslin, straw, felt, etc. Military shapes like classical helmets were very fashionable as also was the turban type. The poke 'Quaker' bonnet remained in fashion with its nodding feathers, ribbons and bows. The deep crown hats set well to the back of the head had deep and open brims. The build-up of the top-knot hair style caused an increase in height with higher crowned hats. Leghorn straw hats were very popular trimmed with ribbon; the ribbons were usually left untied (or loosely tied) a popular fashion fad to be noted by the costume designer. By 1819 the crowns of the hats were made lower with wider brims following the latest hair fashion, smooth and sleek with a centre parting and side puffs and curls. The usual headwear consisted of an indoor cap fastened under the chin over which was worn a large crowned straw hat with a brim (of varying widths) turned off the face on one side and decorated with clusters of ostrich plumes.

Accessories Hand properties of this period, for the costume designer, are the accessories which were either carried or worn. Long gloves to just below elbow-length in various colours, mostly pastel tans, lilac, limerick, stone and lemon were worn for day wear and in the evening white kid with either plain- or ruching-decorated tops. With the long sleeved dresses, short gloves were worn. Handkerchiefs with lace borders were carried and if in mourning these were of black silk. Fans were small and of the folding variety, many of unusual design and often painted.

Muffs were carried and these came in various sizes and materials but were mostly of fur. Often boas and tippets were made to match. Parasols varied in design and came usually in a small size. There were many strange and inventive contraptions attached to the making of the parasols, and

1860s version of an Irish immigrant

29

Straw hat decorated with flowers and ribbon, 1873

these can be seen in museums by designers. The latest fashion of the period was the fringing around the edge of the shade. The umbrella or parapluie was somewhat larger and more bulky and was carried by both men and women. Up to 1820 the long stocking-purse or ridicule, was tucked through the belt or waistband, and was made from many materials. Again the advice to the stage costume designer is to view these articles in the museums which house these collections. They will be astonished at how many of these 'reticules' (another name for them) there are and the number of designs and shapes.

For the *female costume* it was not such an exciting period, one of modification with trimmings rather than a radical upheaval. Until 1820 the predominant colour remained white and the stiff cone and cylinder shapes concealed the natural form.

Men's clothes In the early part of the nineteenth century it will be obvious to the costume designer that the real transition had been in men's costume. The style followed the caprices of the English 'dandies', with their patron, the Prince Regent, later George IV, and George Bryan Brummell (Beau Brummell). This new style was typified by its smartness of cut and fitting, with attention to the merest details. The sombre restraining colouring, buckskin breeches and low-cut boots, tight ankle-buttoned pantaloons, and low, wide-brimmed beaver hats, were accepted and worn by all fashionable and elegant men.

The coat The tail cut-away coat continued as in the previous era for both evening and day wear, cut in single-breasted or double-breasted styles and gradually the double-breasted tail coat became the more fashionable. Unlike the previous era the waistline was cut low and the cut-away tails curved back well over the hips and hung either a little above the back of the knee or were worn long to well below the knee. The coat collar stood high at the back and low in the front and the lapel usually had an M notch or remained plain. The pockets were either secreted in the pleats or were flapped, usually at waist level. Sleeves were close-fitting on the arm but were gathered at the shoulders and generally padded. At the wrist they had a slit and two or three buttons and the stitched-down cuffs came well over the hand. The dandy fashion brought in the use of corsets and padding, the

◄ On the left, the gentleman is in the single-breasted riding habit costume of 1828 complete with a beaver hat. The gentleman on the right is in the double-breasted riding costume of 1850, longer waistcoat and silk top hat

1879 hat style with bird ornamentation

latter often being added to the chest to produce a pigeon-breasted effect. The fashionable colour was light blue for coats adorned with brass buttons or the coats were in sombre tones of black or brown.

Waistcoats were also worn both single- and double-breasted with either a broad or narrow collar. The high, broad, collar was usually supported by thin whalebone ribs sewn into the front edges, the turn-down collar also became fashionable. The bottom edge of the waistcoat was usually cut straight across but the pointed style was also popular. During this period the back of the waistcoat could be drawn in by pairs of tapes. Pockets were not always present, but if worn were usually horizontal slits at waist level, which carried the snuff box (a very popular accessory). The watch was worn hanging on a fob from beneath the waistcoat. Sometimes two waistcoats were worn both for warmth and effect, the upper one cut lower to reveal the top of the underneath waistcoat. Materials consisted of cashmere which was often embroidered, patterned materials, buff kerseymere, swansdown and striped marcella. In 1818 the most fashionable mode was the broad horizontal stripe style, and for evening wear a white piqué was very fashionable from 1814.

Breeches had lengthened and until the beginning of the nineteenth century they reached ankle-length; the lower part at first was hidden by Hessian boots, or top boots, or even gaiters. Later the breeches were worn over the boots and were usually as close-fitting as possible, and were in buckskin or stockinette. Tight-fitting, ankle-length gaiter pantaloons known as 'Moschettos' were worn and by about 1812 trousers (or pantaloons) wider than the gaiter type came into fashion. The Wellington pantaloons style was slit from the calf down and fastened by loops and buttons. From 1819 the pantaloons were secured by straps under the soles of the boots. Various other fashions followed such as straights (the same width down), voluminous 'cossacks', often drawn in at the ankle and these were also pleated at the waistband. Apart from the tight-fitting black pantaloons introduced by Beau Brummell, special trousers were not worn as part of the evening dress until about 1817 and then they came slowly into fashion. Knee-breeches however continued to be worn with the dress coat and at court.

The frock coat, which was to become the most fashionable and popular style of the nineteenth century, was the term given to the long, full-skirted garment of military origin.

1880 revival of the Tudor-style hat

At first it was styled in the single-breasted fashion with either a roll or standing collar, without lapels. The coat was buttoned down the front to the waist and fell vertically to the ground, although the length varied throughout the period. There were various styles and names such as the Polish coat, with its frogging ornamentation, the English redingote with its broad coat tails, and the Wellington frock with the waisted style improving the fall of the skirt.

Outdoor wear   Cloaks were not so fashionable as in the previous century but there was a period in 1809 (a very severe winter) when cloaks of fur were worn by the fashionable dandies. The popular single-breasted great coat was worn and was fastened by either three to four straps down the front, or by buttons; it was usually calf-length with back pleats together with buttons. It had no lapels but had a high standing collar which could be turned down, or with lapels the collar lay flat; collars, cuffs and lapels were often covered with fur. Again there were various styles and names such as the Garrick; a garment with numerous capes in multiple layers often called a Box coat; the Demi-surtout was a low-collared lightweight overcoat; the Polish coat as mentioned above and the Spencer. The latter was an extraordinary fashion. It was a short waist-length coat without tails, and although popular for a while with the men it became more fashionable with the ladies.

Neckwear   At the beginning of the nineteenth century stocks both black and white with a starched collar beneath were worn with a bow in front. As the period progressed the shirt collar rose higher and higher and the neckcloths either had to be more heavily starched or fitted with stiffeners, which became known as choker collars. From about 1818 the neckcloth was shaped at the sides and stiffened with bristles or whalebone to form an arch shape at the cheeks. The cravat was in the form of a scarf and was tied in various ways, each with a different name such as American, Oriental, Horse and Collar, Barrel Knot, Napoleon, Mathematical, Mail Coach and many others.

Hair   Wigs were now worn only at court or by the legal and sometimes the church dignitaries. The hair was cut short but left long enough so that it could be curled. The dishevelled styles of hair dressing of the earlier period were

Close hairstyle brushed away from the face, 1889

now discarded and curls and waves became the fashionable trend. Side whiskers began to make their appearance and were worn by all classes of male society, but moustaches were at this time unfashionable. Because of the high collar fashion, the back hair was usually closer cut to avoid discomfort.

Headwear With the complete disappearance of the three-cornered hat at the beginning of the century, the round hat took over as the most popular headwear throughout Europe, and the top hat made its appearance for fashionable wear. As the top hat gained in popularity it came in various forms, with vertical sides, a flat crown and a narrow brim turned up at the sides; with crowns that narrowed upwards; or the popular style which found great favour around 1819 when the hat widened slightly towards the top. The top hat was to last the whole of the century and into the next in various guises.

Footwear Boots of several varieties including styles from the previous decade were worn. The Hessian boot and the English Jockey boot with the turndown cuff remained in fashion. The usual yellow turndown cuff of the boot was now appearing in other colours such as beige or grey. Boots however were becoming shorter, as they were now being worn under the long trouser leg. Shoes remained unchanged with the exception that buckles were now being replaced by lacing and the buckle style was worn for court and ceremonial occasions only. Gaiters and spatterdashes were popular both in the town and country areas.

Accessories Muffs were still carried by men but whether this was for comfort or affectation it is difficult to say. They were quite large, reaching to the elbow, but from about 1810 they began to decrease both in size and popularity. Both canes and umbrellas were carried and the carrying of riding whips (without a horse) was very popular. Handkerchiefs usually of white linen were now a little smaller, about 4.5 cm (18 in.) square. Men's jewellery consisted mainly of the fob which was of two bars of gold, the top bar being attached to a watch on a swivel and the lower bar having a ring from which a bunch of seals was hung, the fob was then attached to a black moiré ribbon. A quizzing-glass, a small rectangular magnifying glass attached to a handle, or a monocle was carried both for viewing and affectation. At first snuff was very popular but later cigars and smoking became the fashion.

Artificial aids to fashion To improve their figures dandies wore a corset known as an Apollo. Rouge powder, and dyes were extensively used in the name of fashion.

Romantic Period 1820-1837

The age of romanticism, often called the Biedermeier style in Europe was a period when the past and present were juxtaposed; old styles side by side with the innovations of the so-called 'machine-age'. Of interest for both the costume designers and set designers is the levelling of fashion and the recourse to the Gothic and Renaissance style in buildings during this period. This combination resulted in some graceful features but there was also much that was ugly and distasteful. The Romantic movement was influenced by a musical and poetic generation of dreamers, perhaps in defiance of the materialism of the new business classes. It was a period of fashion costume fantasy, reflecting many different influences. Classical, neo-Gothic or neo-Renaissance — each and every style had its followers. Dress styles signified the new middle classes and this was particularly true in the East and Central Europe where people were judged by their costumes. From about 1830 the bourgeoisie set the fashion throughout the western world with the transformation in costume which followed Baroque, Rococo or neo-Gothic tastes, bringing stiffer, more expansive and solemn styles.

The gradual reappearance of the French textile trades on the international market and the exports from the European powers along with the development of the United States with its increase of printed cotton goods, had a marked effect on the growing market of textiles and costume. Technical progress was advanced by Bauwen's loom for woollen goods, Jacquard looms for lace products and one of the greatest milestones was the invention of the sewing machine by the Frenchman Barthélemy Thimmonier (later perfected by Howe and Isaac Singer). The embroidery machine invented by Heilman also helped in increasing industrialization and

1839 young man with side parting

Hat style of 1832 with ribbons and feathers

◄ Fashions of 1829. Both ladies are wearing the off-the-shoulder look with the short full sleeves, normal waistline and full skirt to just above ankle length. The centre lady has a hair-style with ribbons and feathers, the other lady is in the turban headdress. The gentleman is wearing a long overcoat with the full shoulders and wide lapel

production of costume goods. This was the time which saw the beginning of departmental stores for ready-to-wear clothing. Each country adapted foreign fashions to suit its own requirements except in the case of mass-produced items that were imported and which imposed a certain worldwide standard of uniformity.

The term 'Biedermeier style' is derived from a political caricature from the German 'Fliegende Blätter', characterizing all that is sober, plain and simple in form.

An interesting note for theatre designers for purely academic purposes, is the fact that in the 1820s theatres began to replace their candles and oil lamps by gas-light, and by 1830 gas-light was the accepted illumination in urban theatres; this innovation was to have far-reaching consequences resulting in the increased scope of stage effects.

This period was truly an era of invention not only because of the machines which brought improvements to textiles and costume but in other areas. In 1825, for example, George Stephenson's steam locomotive the Rocket travelled from Stockton to Darlington at a speed of twelve miles an hour and by 1835 the telegraph was perfected. There were other inventions too which were responsible for the changes that would fashion the clothes of the future.

Costume however became one of the decorative arts of the Romantic period, and the proliferation of fashion journals provide an abundance of documentation of all the changes that took place during this era. Costume was characterized not by new trends but rather by the bringing back of items from the past. Women laced themselves tighter and tighter and to achieve the wasp-waist the corset reappeared, in this instance not to change the natural line to an artificial shape but merely to slim. As the waistline gradually returned to its natural position the corset became more and more indispensable. It is interesting to note that the number of patents for corsets increased from two in 1828 to 64 just two decades later. They were always in white and seamless, made and woven on the Jacquard looms, sometimes they consisted of a simple belt only. After a period of some 25 years of hygienic sensibility in the art of dressing, fashion demanded constricted shapes once again. At first the lacing was not too conspicuous and the form was controlled by the art of cutting but this did not endure for long and the corset proper returned.

For men, the predominance of black for dress-clothes

Back view of large brimmed bonnet, 1830

became fashionable although blue or brown frock coats were also worn, together with short waistcoats in bright floral designs and neckwear knotted in painstakingly elaborate ways.

The most noticeable thing about women's fashion of this period was the sleeve. The circumference grew to an enormous size with the back looking more than twice as wide as was compatible with the normal proportions of the figure.

Women's fashion From the 1820s the fashionable silhouette was produced by a cone-shaped skirt which over the period gradually widened as more and more petticoats were added. Striped and patterned materials were selected to break up the larger surfaces now being displayed. This fashion also revived styles from the past.

Dresses Although the waistline was still fairly high at the beginning of the period, it gradually dropped until about 1828 when the corseted waistline was back to its natural level, and became the style for all classes. The bodice of the dress had several variations: the draped style had a crossover front with the folds in a variety of arrangements; or the front was straight or pleated or fanwise from the shoulder to the waist forming a squared point. The bodice with the V-shaped front had converging revers, pelerine lapels or pleats known as fichu-robings. The high-necked style of bodice had a narrow turned-down collar or ruff, or a drawstring. At first muslin collars were worn but as the shoulders broadened in 1828 the pelerines increased in size from the neckline with long front tails which tucked into the belt.

The *sleeves* became the most significant feature of the dress. Although small during the first few years they did over the period increase in size. In 1823 the gathered sleeve made its first appearance, the small puff sleeve which had been fashionable for evening wear became unfashionable by 1825 when long sleeves, fully gathered at the shoulders and tapering down to a close-fitting cuff became the vogue for all day and evening wear. By 1827 the sleeves were set lower and the beginning of the sloping shoulder style known as the ham-shaped sleeve was in fashion. With the widening of the former narrow bodice the décolletage increased thus uncovering the neck and upper part of the chest and accentuating the effect of sloping shoulders, which were considered fashionwise to be essential to feminine beauty. The increase

The young lady is wearing an evening dress of 1829 with the puffed shoulder sleeves and laced collar. The skirt is padded at the hem. Gentleman in the peg-topped trouser style and wide brimmed top hat

39

Bonnet with ribbon bows and ties, 1831

Close haircut with beard, 1889

in volume of the sleeve produced such names as gigot or leg-o-mutton, but these were in fact a modification of the six-teenth-century style. Other sleeves came under various names and not least among them was the Imbecile sleeve enormous in size and spread out by pads stuffed with feathers or by linings of stiff buckram. Later these were further distended by means of whalebone hoops or steel hoops. The low-cut boat neckline bared the shoulders and this was worn with the leg-o-mutton or elephant ear (another name) sleeves covered with jockeys, the latter being the Renaissance-inspired round epaulettes at the top of the sleeve. These added width to the shoulders, accentuating the slimness of the waist. This particular silhouette, graceful as it was, soon became lost when the fullness of the sleeve began to fall to the elbow and the wrist, and a cape or shawl hid the bustline to waist level.

The skirt   The real change in women's clothes occurred between 1820 and 1822 with the move from the Classical to the Romantic fashion and with the waist returning to the normal level and becoming tighter and reminiscent of the late eighteenth century. Until 1828 the skirt was flat at the top, gored, fitted smoothly at the front and sides, flaring out towards the feet and ending just above the ankle, re-vealing the pale-coloured stockings and low, thin-soled, flat shoes. From this year, however, the top of the skirt became fuller and was gathered all round into the waist, encased in wide buckled belts. During the period of 1820 to 1828 the lower part of a silk or muslin dress was wadded or padded with cotton-wool. This became a feature of the skirt and as ornamentation and trimming round the hem up to knee level increased, this caused the skirt to stand out. Later, however, this became unfashionable and the decora-tion was reduced to a simple single band of trimming. The evening skirt was usually shorter than the day dress but more profusely decorated at the hem to knee level. The wearing of a separate bodice and skirt, although part of the current fashion, was not at this time very popular.

Day dresses made in muslin, printed cottons, chintz, silk, gingham, batiste, cambric, merino, challis and levantine, were usual, but silks, satins, gauze and organdy were used for evening dresses. Piping on dresses, especially those made in muslin, came in about 1822 and became more fashionable in later years. The use of pastel shades and blending of

Lady in a ball gown costume of 1830. The full shoulder sleeves are beginning to droop over the shoulders. The skirt is full and padded at the hem. A pelerine is worn

various colours was very popular and striped materials were used for evening wear. White still remained most popular; flowered designs in pinks, blues, yellows, reds, greens and lilac were often seen.

Centre parting with side curls decorated with hair combs

Rear view of the 1830 hair-style with hair comb

On his ascent to the throne in 1820, George IV abolished the eighteenth-century style hoop from the court ceremonial female dress, and the new costume was modelled on the lines of those adopted by the French court under Louis XVIII.

From 1820 onwards women's fashionable neckwear followed the historical broad neckruff sometimes called a fraise. About 1827 the ruff was replaced with a flat shoulder-cape with a narrow frill at the top. The chemisette, tucker, falling tucker and the ruff were all in fashion at this time. Delicate coloured cravats and scarves in gauze and silk were often worn. Also worn were long stoles, pelerines (wide flat collars covering the shoulders and the bosom) and the fichu-pelerine which made its appearance in 1826. This was a pelerine with tails which fell down the front and tucked through the belt, sometimes hanging almost to the knees. Still maintaining its popularity since the beginning of the period was the fichu-shaped chemisette, worn with a low-necked bodice, the canezou.

Ourdoor garments were silk cloaks or mantles, in various forms and these were popular in shoulder or waist lengths. Colourful shawls were more commonly worn by the older ladies. Tippets were popular and fur tippets were used in the winter.

Headwear After 1822 hats began to overtake bonnets in the field of fashion, brims were turned up and the hat was worn to one side and in 1827 the fashion was for one or two ribbons dangling down behind as far as the waist. Materials were crêpe, satin, straw or velvet with feathers round the crown and often an excessive ornamentation of bows, flowers and ribbons under the brim. Large flat berets and turbans loaded with feathers were also in fashion. After 1829 costume was very much inspired by the Renaissance, and hair was built up with plaits and curls. Caps with names like 'à la dona Maria', and 'Alsatain' wide flat berets were worn, at an almost vertical angle. For evening wear came the chaperon of feathers or a petit bord: a hat also inspired by the Renaissance period, which enjoyed a long spell in fashion.

Footwear Heelless shoes or pumps followed the styles of the earlier period and remained unchanged until about 1830, when the eighteenth-century style of square toe returned to fashion. Boots and gaiters were worn for travelling and

1830 style of hairdressing. Hair brushed up from a centre parting

Back view of hairstyle

Centre parting with side puff ▶ curls

inclement weather, and the boots were usually laced down the sides. Black satin shoes were popular for evening wear and dancing. Silk or cotton stockings were worn, black for evening, grey for day wear. Clogs had leather tops and cork soles and heels. Even at this time shoes were not shaped for either left or right feet.

Hairstyles changed with fashion. Popular during this period was the plait fixed to the back of the head with a comb of horn or tortoiseshell. It was considered very fashionable to wear ringlets at the side of the face, it was also fashionable to wear dyed red silk 'curls' which hung in two puffs from the forehead and were secured by a band tied round the head. These side puffs could be purchased to match the hair, and were useful to dress the hair with the minimum of effort, as hairdressing salons were not as yet common practice. Young ladies wore the simple lovelock style behind the ears. Some women however remained faithful to the curls of the previous decade well into the 1820s, allowing the costume designer a certain latitude in the overlapping of styles. The new style for this period was the centre parting and the hair scraped flat across the top of the head with the sides arranged in falling ringlets. Later in the 1820s the hairstyles became gradually higher and by 1830 they had reached absurd proportions being supported by wire frames, ornamental pins and decorated with feathers, ribbons or flowers.

This extreme hairdo was already outmoded by 1835 and although of the same basic design it became lower, the top-knot, now a mere braided hairpiece, worn high at the back of the head.

Artificial aids to beauty were very few. Rouge remained the mode until about 1837 when a white pallor was thought to be more interesting and romantic.

Accessories Although most of these are part of the costume, quite a few of these items could well be hand properties. Coloured gloves were worn for day use, in doeskin or cotton, green-coloured gloves being most fashionable. With the advent of the long sleeve, the short glove was more popular. Evening gloves however were long to the elbow and usually in white kid. Handkerchiefs edged in lace were carried in the hand.

Aprons were popular accessories but were worn without bibs and made in gauze and muslin. Reticules, bags and sachets still continued in fashion and were in coloured silks, tulle, chenille, satin and velvet, often with drawstrings or cord handles. Later, new shapes with tortoiseshell or steel clasps became popular. The carrying of bouquets was all the rage and these were also tucked into the décolletage. Fans were essential to fashion. They were small, often of hand-painted silk and were mounted on wood or mother-of-pearl handles; some fans were made of feathers. Muffs at the beginning of the period were on the large side but later began to decrease in dimensions. They were made from fur or feathers and ornamented in front by a bow.

Parasols changed little from the preceding period and the fashion to have them just dangling in the hand without opening them, was considered very chic. The women at this time wore a great deal of jewellery, both real and fake. Some more elegant women even brought back into fashion reminiscences of the past, for example, the ferronière a fine chain with a pearl on the forehead, as worn during the Renaissance.

Men The male world of fashion was centred in London, and the fashionable people of Europe and America followed it as faithfully as possible in the English manner. The most popular of the undress coats was the frock coat, which had at this time assumed its basic shape which, with only minor

Bonnet with silk back piece, 1835

44

modifications, was to remain the same throughout the century. Although usually double-breasted it was also fashionable to have the single-breasted version. It was close-fitting to the waist, flaring out in folds to reach knee level; after 1830 it became shorter to just below hip level. The rolling collar had a V or M notch, with lapels to almost waist level. At first the sleeves were full at the shoulders and gathered en gigot, after 1832 they ceased to be gathered and became long and close-fitting to the wrist with a slit cuff.

Waistcoats were now longer waisted and until 1830 were in the single-breasted style which was very much in favour. They had a slight dip in front and were known as the Hussar style. The usual waistcoat had a rolled collar and lapel which reached to just below mid-chest. When the double-breasted waistcoat became fashionable again, it too had a rolled collar often faced with a different material to the rest of the garment. Materials were cashmere, sprigged marcella, spotted valencia, striped toilinette, and nankin. Often the more extreme fashion had starkly harsh bright colours with broad purple, salmon and crimson stripes. For evening wear white marcella or black velvet waistcoats were worn. About 1830 most waistcoats, both for day and evening wear had the shawl type collar.

Breeches were still worn for ceremonial court occasions. For all other occasions the pantaloons were worn, these being secured under the foot by a strap or with side slits and worn with half boots like Hessians. Trousers, referred to at this time as pantaloon-trousers were also strapped under the foot or buttoned up by a side slit and for evening wear the strap came under the stocking. The Cossack pantaloons were now less full than previously and were close-fitting to the ankle. Embroidered braces of silk on a canvas backing made their appearance in 1831.

The costume designer of this period need have no excuses for lack of colour, the later sombreness of the nineteenth century was not yet in evidence. The fashionable dandies tried to evoke some sense of colour eg a light tan coat, a sky-blue satin and violet waistcoat, off-white nankin pantaloons, yellow stockings with violet clocks and buckled shoes could be worn.

Neckwear continued as in the previous decade high in the neck with excessive starching, in a variety of hues. Collars

◄ The evening dress of the lady for 1834 has the full gigot sleeve ending closely at the wrist. The man is dressed in the French style of the period with the pelisse coat and shawl collar

were still high above the stocks. In 1830 the frilled shirt front was becoming unfashionable and plain shirts were more commonly worn. For evening wear white was still essential.

For undress wear negligées, dressing- and morning-gowns and banyans were very fashionable. The banyan was a long-waisted coat with flared skirts almost reaching the ground.

Outdoor garments were greatcoats in both single- and double-breasted styles. The collars were worn with or without lapels, often faced with fur. Pockets were either flapped or placed in the pleats. Sleeves were slightly gathered at the shoulders, long with buttoned cuffs. The surtout greatcoat was a fashionable close-fitting garment and the Wellington coat which appeared about 1828 was similar in style and cut to the frock coat. The Box-coat with one or more cape-like deep collars was still very popular as was the Spencer coat which remained unchanged. Cloaks for both day and evening wear were usually long and voluminous. Shawls were worn over all garments for travelling.

Sport attire for riding, shooting and hunting was very fashionable, and a closer study of the garments worn would be

Front view of toque, 1830

Back view of feather and silk toque

well worthwhile. Although similar to the other costumes of the period there are obvious differences, some are shown in the illustrations.

Still popular as *footwear* were boots, top-boots, Hessians, Wellingtons and Bluchers. The square-toed variety continued to be worn, but pointed-toed shoes and boots were very fashionable in 1829. Buckled shoes were worn less and lace-up shoes and boots were becoming more fashionable.

Headwear The top hat remained the most popular and commonly worn headgear, as it was to remain for the rest of the century. The crown of the hat was very high with the narrow brim curled up at the sides. Black, fawn or white beaver or felt was used. Low crowned hats with extra large brims were usually worn by the country people. An unusual style for this period (although it was the prototype for a future popular hat) was a bowl-shaped hat worn about 1821. Caps were worn for sport or in the house.

Hairstyles Curls were fashionable as hairstyles with a centre or side parting. Although cut close to the head the hair was by no means short. The earlier trend was to be cleanshaven but by 1825 the French fashion of having side whiskers was allowed to increase until they formed a fringe around the face. In 1835 working men who usually wore their hair long had semi-curls at either side which were called aggravators.

Accessories Gloves were now an essential part of fashion and were worn by both sexes in doeskin, silk and cotton in a variety of colours. The carrying of handkerchiefs was still a fashionable trend among the dandies. Canes and umbrellas were carried and the stems and stocks were often carved with ingenious skill.

Male *jewellery* consisted of snuff boxes and eyeglass pieces with gold frames, worn with a black ribbon. Gold watches and seals were carried by the more wealthy citizens.

Short hair and vandyke beard, 1894

Fashion followed the same trends throughout the western world. On the left, the male fashion of the 1840s. Centre, a lady at the height of fashion of the 1890s and right, following the tradition of their African heritage, the type of clothes that could be worn by a female American slave of the 1860s

The nineteenth century began the trend for more sombre colours for male fashion and in contrast were the colourful uniforms of the armies of Europe. Left, a Regimental Sergeant Major of the Highland Light Infantry, 1897. Centre, an early nineteenth century uniform of a Westphalian Garde du Corps officer. Right, a Prussian officer of the Garde du Corps, 1845

Early Victorian 1837-1857

This period is sometimes called the Second Rococo, because of its superficial resemblance to that period, and by the French it is known as the Second Empire. Whatever its name it was an era of great material and scientific progress.

It was during this period that the rebirth of the crinoline and the polonaise occurred and this was typical of a century where inspiration was sought from the past. Both these styles had enjoyed great popularity during the First Rococo under Louis XVI. Many of these fashions were brought back only to disappear and reappear a decade or so later under a different name. Such is the world of fashionable costume and for the costume designer, once he has recognized the basic dress of the century, it is not too difficult to understand the vagaries of fashion throughout the period being studied.

The problems of research for the designer of today are greatly helped by the inventive processes of that time. Photography was making its first appearance through a theatrical scene painter, Louis Jacques Mandé Daguerre (1789-1851). Whilst attempting a method to simplify the reproduction of the images in his diorama (a new type of pictorial exhibition in which panoramic views were shown in succession and illuminated by special lighting effects) he developed a method of printing a picture by the action of sunlight. This was developed into the Daguerreotype, being the exposure to light of a sensitized plate coated with iodide of silver, then 'fixed' by the action of mercury vapour and hyposulphite of soda. Fashion plates were enhanced by this method and proved adequate until more modern photography was introduced some years later, allowing fashion modes to be seen in journals and newspapers.

The growing industrialization of this epoch forced a great increase in the importation of silks, cottons and wool which in turn were processed and exported as finished goods. In 1856 the Englishman Sir William Henry Perkin (1838-1907) discovered the first synthetic dyestuff: aniline coal-tar dye. It was called aniline purple, a tone which could not be obtained by the use of natural dyes. Later synthetic dyes gradually replaced all natural dyes.

Women's fashion The chief characteristic of women's costume in the mid-nineteenth century was the large circumference at the base of the dress. The horsehair petticoats

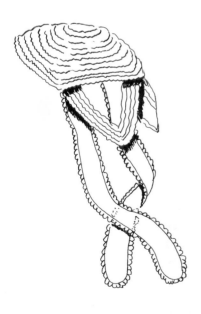

Swiss muslin cap, 1871

Muslin breakfast cap, 1871

Lady in morning dress of 1842 with close-fitting waist and open bodice, tight sleeves and flounced skirt. Gentleman in a walking costume tail coat

Promenade dress of 1838. The lady is in the ankle length, full gathered skirt, wide brimmed bonnet with bavolet and pelerine mantlet. The morning coat of the gentleman is close-fitting to the waist and the pantaloons are strapped under the shoes

Tall hat with bird ornamentation, 1887

Longer hair and sideboards style, 1864

with further padded petticoat garments, and stiffly starched underskirts all contributed to this effect and they became progressively wider from the 1850s with the introduction of the hooped cages which took the name of crinolines.

The bodice continued in the late thirties, as in the previous decade, with the pointed, longer style, with the back fastening being the most popular. The V-shape pleating and the wide low décolletage were both in fashion. The bodice was now stiffened with bone supports spreading up in a fan shape from the waist. The jacket bodice and the gilet corsage styles were close-fitting and fastened down the front from the neck to the waist, the former style ending in short basquins, often being worn with a separate skirt. The bodices of the fifties were usually open down the centre to the waist, revealing a lace or muslin chemisette. By the late fifties the boned bodice with the back fastening became unfashionable and the front-fastening jacket gained in popularity. This was close-fitting to the waist with short basquins along with the caraco bodice and long basques coming over the hips. By the forties sleeves for day wear dresses were fitting tight to the wrist often with a small bell-shaped expansion below the elbow and washable white half-sleeves ending in closed cuffs or frills called engageantes, which were secured by ties inside the sleeve. By the fifties the sleeves were made shorter, often wide revealing the frilled undersleeves. A puffed style undersleeve was very popular.

The skirts during the thirties became wider, their width increased by more and more petticoats, and small pads placed under the back pleating. By 1846 the long full skirt was gathered into the waist by organ pleating consisting of a tubular type of pleat, hence its name. This, along with the horsehair petticoat and padding, gave a domed silhouette shape. Flounces were the popular skirt ornamentation and made the skirt flare out at the hem from the corseted waist. By about 1856 there was a decrease in the number of petticoats worn by inserting steel hoops above the hem. In the following year a contraption appeared in the shape of a cage or hooped skirt (crinoline) made from fine steel hoops graduated some 7-10 cm (3 to 4 in.) apart, being tied by tapes from the waist. In front it was left open by gaps in the upper hoops to allow the garment to be put on. This fashion of wide skirts extending some 3-4 m (12 to 15 ft) in circumference was adopted by all classes. Although the styles were fairly numerous, plain skirts were not so popular for

Bustle jacket style 1885

Cuirass style of 1877

the more fashionable set. Materials for the dresses were usually silks, moiré, foulard, poplin and taffeta. For evening wear organdy, muslin and brocades were very fashionable. The mechanical substructures of the dress were rolls of horsehair with petticoats and later the metal cage contraption which was attached to the waist by ties that fastened in the front.

Neckwear   Collars were generally in vogue with the sleeves following the earlier fashion of the broad collar with large sleeves. Later came the close-fitting sleeve and a narrower collar. A jacket-like chemisette of muslin was worn under the bodice and was sometimes called a canezou or often a fichu.

Outdoor garments   Cloaks and mantles remained in various fashionable styles. The full three-quarter length mantle was shaped to the waist in front but more loosely fitted at the back. The shawl, known as a pelerine was popular from about 1837 to the early forties. This short cape shawl, usually made of silk with its long ends falling down the front, was by 1844 called a mantelet écharpe. After 1850 wraps became shorter with less padding, for summer wear they were made from silks and in winter they were of cloth and velvet. The Burnous mantle was generally worn for evening attire, it had a hood and was ornamented with frogging and fastened from a V neck to the waist. The Talma mantle was again a full cloak with a flat collar (or hood) often called a Rotonde. The Pelisse mantle was a double-breasted loose overcoat with a flat collar and short, wide sleeves. Close-fitting jackets with tight sleeves were also in vogue, finely embroidered in the eighteenth-century style.

Headwear   Small caps worn at the back of the head often had lappets whilst others had long flowing ribbons hanging down behind. By 1855 these were often replaced by twists of ribbons. There were many varieties of hats and bonnets worn during this period. The early bonnets had fairly wide brims tied under the chin, framing the face. The straw bonnet with a straight poke was popular during the forties. By 1853, the bonnets had considerably reduced in size with the introduction of frills round the back and sides. These frills often large and stiffened with buckram were called bavolets. In nearly all cases the bonnets were secured on the head by ribbons tied under the chin, although the younger fashionable element left these ribbons untied and allowed to hang down on either side. These were known as brides. A close-fitting bonnet called a capote was very fashionable during the forties and flowers and feathers were the usual decoration for all bonnets. Although the plain straw hat was worn by the country people for a long period of time it was during this time that the fashionable world took up this trend of straw hats. In 1854 the large straw hat called a

Lady in a day dress of the 1850s with a basquin jacket bodice with a multiple flounced skirt over a crinoline case frame. Narrow bonnet worn at the back of the head with ribbon strings. Small boy with full-skirted dress, laced pants and round peaked cap

Neat close hairstyle of the 1900s

Off-the-face style 1900

round hat, not to be confused with the male version, was a large flat mushroom shape with the low crown decorated with flowers and ribbons. In 1857 the mousquetaire hat made its appearance, a smaller version of the round hat with the addition of a narrow lace curtain placed round the edge of the brim. Veils were now becoming very fashionable.

Hairstyles The centre parting style prevailed throughout the period and was worn for both day and evening. The hair came down from the parting on either side and was dressed in a number of different ways: plaited, then drawn up into a circle to surround the ears, or turned up from the covered ears to be incorporated in the back knot or bun. Another style was to allow the hair to hang in ringlets down the back or either side of the shoulders.

Footwear Heelless slipper-type shoes were worn for all formal occasions. Boots which often matched the dress or elastic-sided boots were worn. Evening wear was usually satin heelless slipper shoes.

Accessories Gloves were of the short variety in coloured kid or cotton and usually buttoned. Mittens made of silk were also worn. Handkerchiefs were carried and these were fairly large and edged with lace. Reticules were now becoming old-fashioned with the advent of pockets in the skirts. Fans were always carried and these were at this period of a medium size and of the folding variety. The carrying of a muff was very fashionable and this was made from fur, sometimes with a matching fur boa. Parasols were now small, fringed and often embroidered.

Men's costume As from 1840 the tail coat was worn for all occasions, in both the single- and double-breasted styles. The frock coat however dominated the fashionable scene for men, it was now close-fitting with a long waist and short skirts. The frock was worn with or without lapels, and if lapels were present they had a V or M notch. But already by 1850 the M notch was becoming unfashionable. The sleeves were close-fitting with a small cuff, or slit with buttons. Introduced for this fashion was a breast pocket worn on the left side. The riding coat was often used as a walking coat. The single-breasted hip-length jacket with a small collar and lapels

Straw bonnet with flower and feather decoration, 1887

Wide brimmed straw hat with flowers 1889

was popular fashion wear.

Waistcoats These were now being worn in longer styles than in the previous decade, they were usually single-breasted with rolled lapels and could be buttoned to the neck in winter. Bright colours in striped materials were still fashionable among the more trendy fashion addicts. In the forties and the fifties flowered designs and tartan were popular. After 1855 waistcoats started to become shorter.

Trousers were closer-fitting and worn with under-the-foot straps. Popular still were trousers pleated at the waist (the previous cossack type) wide at the hips and tapering towards the ankle. Trouser materials were usually cloth, merino, doeskin and plaid, often in bright colours.

Neckwear Large bows, often with pointed ends worn over a cravat were the most common, but as with all fashion there were various styles with numerous names attached to them.

Negligée dressing gowns remained very much as they were in previous decades. In 1852 the velvet smoking jacket with the frogging ornamentation was introduced.

Outdoor garments These had various names and were cut in various ways. The frock, greatcoat, overcoat, top frock were in evidence and the styles carried such names as Chesterfield, Pilot coat, Driving coat, and the wrapper. In 1857 the Raglan cape was introduced, made at first in a waterproof material. Cloaks often just above knee-length had a turnover collar.

Footwear The popular high boot again came under various names such as top-boot, Napoleon and Wellington. The half boots to which the popular Hessian style belonged were no longer as fashionable. Boots with elastic sides were worn almost throughout the period. Gaiters and spatterdashes were worn both in the country and the towns.

Headwear The top hat still remained the most popular headwear. The low-crown 'wide awake' hat came in various forms of felt and straw. The Bollinger was an early version of the bowler. Both fur and peaked caps were in common usage.

Hair The current fashion for the male hairstyle was a close curly appearance with side whiskers. Moustaches were now fashionable following the military style from the Crimean War in 1857.

Accessories Gloves, short and plain yellow or buff were the vogue. Long and short canes and black or brown umbrellas were carried.

Mid-Victorian 1857-1877

This was a period of great importance in the history of the world, wars followed a seemingly unending pattern throughout. In Europe conflicts between nations disturbed the political and economic structures of the warring participants. Britain and France declared war on Russia in support of Turkey in 1853 and this ended with the peace treaty of Paris in 1856. From this the fashion world inherited the Raglan and the Cardigan both of which were to survive until the present day. In America the Southern states seceded in 1860, but were finally defeated by the North in 1865. The American Civil War was the first so-called 'modern' war. Many costume innovations came from this conflict. From July of 1870 came the Franco-Prussian War with all its appalling ramifications for France, ending in a peace treaty in 1871. The collapse of the Second French Empire under Napoleon III caused the temporary abdication of France as the leader of worldwide feminine fashion. In 1876 she regained her position with the showing of complete collections of costumes at the Centennial Exposition of Philadelphia in the United States.

This period saw the establishment of two very important trends for costume history: firstly the governing of fashion by general economic conditions prevalent at the time and not merely by political or court influences and secondly the introduction and appearance of couture which was a manifestation of the taste and creativity of individuals. The Englishman Charles Frederick Worth revolutionized the standard of cut and style and displayed his designs on live models for the first time. His name is associated with the elegant French Empress Eugénie whose costumes he designed and made and the term Haute Couture was born.

An interesting and important distinction which the stage costume designer should bear in mind for this era is the increasing difference between clothes of the wealthier upper and middle class and the working class. This perhaps had

Special war correspondent on active service, 1876

The American Civil War of 1860. A freed negro slave in a greatcoat of the period and soldiers in the uniform worn during the hostilities

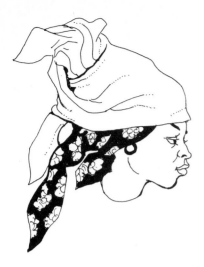

American negro girl with double head-covering, 1860

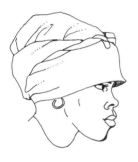

Head cloth of negro girl slave

Simple head cloth at the back of the head

always existed but in this time of greater democracy it was highlighted by the couture system for the privileged.

The Second Empire was, however, the beginning of the time when reasonably priced luxury goods came within the reach of those of humbler origins living in the towns and countryside and no longer were they for the exclusive use of the upper classes and the nouveaux riches.

A typical feature of the period was the use of dyestuffs. Although great strides had been made in their production, the poor retaining quality of many of these dyes made the speedy replacement of costumes essential and this helped to persuade the general public to dress in the fashionable vogue of the day.

Women's fashion The bodice of the dress during this period varied from time to time in being either long and pointed or round, finishing with a waistband. It could often be a different material from the skirt, forming a separate bodice and skirt. The bodice could also be buttoned up close to the neck or with a V-shape or square neckline, revealing a chemisette. The constant factor however throughout the period was the tightly boned waist. Blouse chemisettes of lace or muslin, the bertha and the jacket bodice were all very popular. In 1861 the Garibaldi shirt became very popular with the younger fashionable females. These shirts followed the style worn by Giuseppe Garibaldi, 1807-1882, the hero

Spectacular head cloth

59

of the Italian uprising to unite Italy in 1859. It was a blouse of a bright scarlet French merino, with a narrow collar, the whole blouse being trimmed with black braid and worn with a small narrow black cravat. Worn sometimes over the blouse was a Zouave jacket — à la Zouave — but always with a black silk close-fitting skirt. The casaque, a close-fitting jacket bodice appeared time and again during the period, as did the Corsage Postillion. Sleeves of both the loose- and tight-fitting variety were worn, usually with deep shoulder epaulettes. There were several styles, Bishop, Manderin and Pagoda, to mention a few, which were the open or loose sleeve style. The coat sleeve type were close-fitting sleeves with a tight wrist ending.

The full skirts depending on the crinoline structure continued in fashion in various guises. From the dome shape of the previous decade they spread outwards to the large, wide base dresses of the 1860s. These often reached some 5 m (18 ft) in circumference, with names like à la Pompadour or à la Watteau.

By the late sixties, however, the fullness of the dress was removed and the skirts were gored to fit the figure at the waist, although still wide at the hem. The circular crinoline shape was decreasing in popularity. The new vogue between 1865 and 1870 was the Dolly Varden style, a revival of an eighteenth-century fashion of a long plain skirt with a flounced hem over which was worn a pointed bodice; the back was a bunched up polonaise-style over a bustle. This brought about new metal contraptions. The silhouette was now a flat front skirt with a curved back and a full protruding posterior. By 1869 most dresses had double skirts with large bouffant shapes at the back and the upper skirt was caught up at the sides forming an apron effect in the front called a tablier. The skirts at this period were now invariably trained. The materials used were usually medium-lightweight.

Outdoor garments The three-quarter length cloaks continued to be fashionable in various styles with a variety of sleeve modifications. Shawls which were very popular were usually large and oblong in shape and fringed. The female overcoat was called the paletot again in various forms, being in both the single- and double-breasted styles, and worn both long and short.

Headwear The style of bonnets continued as in the previous era until about 1860 when a new and higher shape came into fashion. This was popularly known as the spoon-bonnet, due to the growing height of the bonnet, inside was a space filled with lace and flowers, a bavolet was added at the nape of the neck. A study by the costume designer of the fashion journals of this time will clearly show that hats were now more popular than bonnets. Many of these hats are included in the illustrations along with their names.

Hairstyles   The hairstyles prevailing were more or less in a similar mode to the previous decade. The early sixties saw the introduction of the chignon, this being enclosed in a net. The chignon dominated the period and could be worn low on the nape of the neck, sausage-shape, or round-shaped with many curls down the back. These styles were frequently adorned with flowers, lace and ribbons. False hair was often added built over pads. About 1870 the front and sides of the hair were waved close to the head with a chignon at the back.

Footwear   Shoes were now worn with both square- and rounded-toes with the addition of 2.5 cm (1 in.) high heels. Boots reaching well above the ankle, were both laced and elasticated and came in various colours and decoration.

Accessories   Still an essential feature of being well dressed was the wearing of gloves. They were short to the wrist, great consideration being given to their fit and shape for fashionable wear. They were often beautifully embroidered. Evening gloves to elbow-length were more popular. Aprons were still worn as part of the overall dress but were now much smaller and called fig leaves. Handbags had lost some favour and were not carried by the ultra-fashionable female. Large fans were carried as also were small muffs. Up to the end of the decade boas of fur were extremely fashionable.

Men's costume   The male styles were now approaching a more relaxed and easier vogue. The frock coat although similar to the previous decade was no longer waisted and the skirts of the coat hung down with flare or fullness. By 1869, short frock coats became very fashionable. The lounging jacket and the morning coat were now being worn with the single-breasted style being the most fashionable. Also about this time was the double-breasted reefer or pea-jacket

Back view of frock coat fashion, 1888

Male fashions of 1900. On the right is the sleeveless caped Ulster and on the left, the double-breasted Ulster riding costume

Two examples of the male fashion of the mid 1860s. Left, the double-breasted knee length frock coat. On the right the shorter version just below hip length with single-breasted waistcoat, bowler hat and the then popular 'Dundreary whiskers'

which was one of the many types of jackets being worn at this time.

Waistcoats were now being cut straight across the bottom and were short-waisted and worn always with single-breasted jackets.

Trousers were becoming closer fitting from 1865 and were made with fly-fronts and until 1876 the legs were narrow and straight. Knickerbockers based on the style of the earlier breeches worn by the military, were now very popular for country and sportswear.

Neckwear High neckwear was now in the process of being replaced by stiffened collars which came in several varieties being stand-up, turned-down or standing with the corners turned. The necktie also received some attention and was now stiffened with a reinforced lining.

Outdoor garments   The popular style of overcoats were now the Chesterfield, the Albert, Paletot, Raglan, Ulster, Inverness cape and the Gladstone.

Headwear   The top hat was still the most popular form of headwear, but now creeping into fashion were soft and hard felt hats as high bowlers, low bowlers, helmet hats and high and low straw hats.

Accessories   Gloves maintained their position in fashion and were always worn; they were usually plain and made in kid or doeskin. Small muffatees and wrist muffs were often carried in winter.

Centre figure is wearing the single-breasted frock coat of 1865. The man on the left is in the wrap-over sleeved loose overcoat just below hip-length, of 1850, and the man on the right is wearing the single-breasted frock coat and checked trousers of 1865

Lady on the right is in the fashion of the late 1860s wearing the double skirt with a bustle and puffs. On the left is a lady in the fashion of 1876 with the 'cuirass' bodice style. The skirt was worn with an apron front and was trained

◄ Lady in a travelling costume with the full skirt and large, loose cloak shawl with the tasselled ends. Narrow bonnet with ribbon ties worn well back on the head. The man is wearing the naval uniform of the 1860s with the small naval hat

Late Victorian 1877-1900

The last two decades of the nineteenth century were the forerunner of the great things to come. Whilst it is impossible to go into all the details of the changes which occurred in this period, we can at least give one last lingering look at the 'Gilded Age'.

Working woman's costume of
1887

 The fashions of 1884-85 show
the introduction of the bustle
style. On the left is the redin-
gote-mantle-edged and decorated
with beaver fur. On the right is
the high-necked closed bodice
with the hitched-up bustle effect

As far as costume was concerned it became apparent
that through the haute couture influence of the French
fashion houses, female costume, that is, French-influenced
costume became the predominant feature of European-
style garments throughout the world. It not only developed
a formula for dress but also a way of life, a manifestation
for the wealthier anyway, of dress and manners.

Although the cab, landaus, broughams and the bicycle
were still, apart from the railway, the only means of transport, the newfangled horseless carriage — the motor car —
was already being manufactured. This in itself was to bring
about profound changes that would also affect the world
of costume.

The 1890s saw the first real signs of women's emancipation,
not politically at this stage, but in the development of sport
such as tennis, cycling, boating and fencing. Strangely enough
this did nothing to lessen the big gulf between the classes.
The wearing of sports costume was at this time a mark of
wealth.

The theatre as a medium of entertainment not only
influenced fashionable costume through the clothes worn
by the actresses and actors, but also seriously concerned
itself with many social problems through dramatic literature.

As the nineteenth century started, so it finished with war
and talk of war. Both the old and the new worlds were in
various states of conflict as far afield as China, South Africa,
Cuba and the Philippines.

Women's costume The last period of the nineteenth
century was seen as a struggle between fashions. Both the
bodice joined to the skirt and the separate bodice and skirt
styles continued to be worn. The high to the neck front
fastening bodice which was shaped to the tightly constricted
waist was not so popular as the square or V-shape front with
the fill-in chemisette. The jacket bodice with the corsage
postillion was popular with many variations. Towards the end
of the period the bodice was lined and boned similar to the
corset with a standing collar, the waist was either pointed
or round, sometimes short basques were present. The loose
blouse as a separate top made its first appearance in 1877
and was in contrast to the tightly corseted style. It was hip
length and secured by a belted skirt, it also had various
names and styles. A brilliant American illustrator was a great
influence with his drawings of the typical young American

67

girl. Charles Dana Gibson (1867-1944) had in 1892 created the Gibson Girl a style which became the vogue throughout Europe and America. It showed the less confining and more comfortable waist shirt and skirt fashion with a narrow turned-down collar and puffed sleeves, worn with a stiff flaring skirt. The male style Norfolk bodice jacket also appeared in 1877, ending at hip level and made of a heavier material, often worn with a pleated, trained skirt.

In the seventies sleeves were wide at the wrist in the pagoda fashion. From about 1880 they were closer fitting with a small kickup gigot at the shoulder, this style lasted until about 1893. By 1895 the shoulder width had extended and the silhouette was a massive shoulder form. This fashion however was very short-lived and disappeared entirely in 1897. From then until the end of the period the sleeves were close-fitting and worn with and without the puffed shoulder sleeve effect.

The skirt during this period was at first double with the bustle becoming smaller. The outline now was of a skirt flattened at the front with tape-ties inside the under skirt that could manipulate the overskirt drapery, upwards, downwards and sideways. By 1878, however, the fullness was taken out of the skirt and the skirt now became close-fitting to the body falling to the ground with a train. These styles were known as princess and polonaise, both styles being very popular and fashionable.

From about 1887 the bustle also disappeared along with the wire and stuffed contraptions. The double skirt with its draperies lost favour about 1894 and its place was taken by the gored skirt which was made to fit the hips and flared from the knees to ground level. With almost each new modification came different names such as umbrella skirt, empire skirt, sun-ray skirt and many others.

Outdoor garments Because of the exaggerated sleeve fashion in the last decade cloaks and mantles were usually worn, often with a wired stand-up collar, which was very popular. Tailored coats were now all the rage and from 1892 the male fashion of the Chesterfield was commonly worn. The coats were either long to the ground or three-quarter length and were both single- and double-breasted. Popular towards the end of the period was the short, open, figure-fitting jacket which reached the knees and had broad revers and large sleeves.

1889 frock coat with single-breasted waistcoat

Dayclothes of 1888 are shown here. The lady is in a plain fronted dress with a sash belt.

The sleeveless cape was large enough to accommodate the straw-filled bustle at the back.

The man is wearing the ever fashionable double-breasted frockcoat and silk topper

Young lady in princess-line sailor costume, 1876

Lady in an evening gown of 1894 with a pointed waist, draped across the bust, and fur shoulder straps. The skirt is flat in front with a train. The gentleman is in the traditional evening dress costume with stepped lapel

Headwear Small bonnets and toques with ribbon and flowered ornamentation were still fashionable. In 1895 pleated brims and larger hats made their appearance. The masculine designed Homburg felt hat was worn both for dress wear and sport activity.

Hairstyles The hair was cut close to the head with fullness at the front, and a curly frizz over the forehead. From 1897 the hair was dressed back from the forehead and the back hair pulled up and worn high.

Footwear Shoes which had followed the fashion of the previous decade with low heels were now increasing in height with the round-toed fashion continuing. Boots were either laced or buttoned and in 1898 they followed the American fashion of pointed-toes.

70

1870, double-breasted frock coat

Male hair and moustache mode 1868

Accessories Gloves still maintained their importance as a fashionable accessory being short and grey or tan in colour. For evening wear they were usually long and in suede or silk. Handbags of various designs were carried as were muffs of both the large and small styles. Fans were again larger than the previous decades and were made of feathers. Boas were still popular and made from fur or feathers. Parasols, carried throughout the period were still fairly tall with carved handles of wood or china. The tops were of silk or chiffon with lace frilled borders.

Men's fashions The male clothing followed the previous styles very closely with certain modifications. The dress coat appeared in 1882 with the lapels faced with a corded silk and by 1884 became tightly fitting at the waist. The lounge dress became known as the dinner jacket in 1888. For a short time the frock coat lost its popularity but by 1889 was back in favour with a higher waistline. Various forms of morning jackets were in fashion with the sportive reefer and Norfolk jackets. Harris Tweed was a very popular material for jackets.

Waistcoats With the popularity of wearing single-breasted jackets, waistcoats were revealed more than previously and were now longer and often produced in striking materials. The fashion by 1888 was to make both the jacket and the waistcoat in the same material. By the end of the century they were being made for almost every occasion, golf, racing, and for all other sport and dress occasions. They varied from plain checks to highly decorated patterns. The cummerbund made its appearance in about 1893, first in black for evening wear then later in colours for morning wear also, the fashion then disappeared to reappear in a much later era.

Trousers These varied only in width being narrow bottoms, tight at the knee and wider bottoms. By 1896 the peg-tops with a wide knee and a narrow turn-up bottom, became the fashion. In 1895 the English method of ironing a crease down the front of each trouser leg became the new fashion.

Neckwear With the high-buttoned waistcoats, the neckwear had little chance of change. But the fashionable collar increased in size to between 5-7 cm (2-3 in.) by about 1899, and came in many variations.

Outdoor garments The Chesterfield remained the most fashionable overcoat in 1896 and was often worn long to knee-length. The top frock was still worn and was long to the ankle. The Ulster coat, very popular for late autumn and winter was made with either a cape or hood attachment. The covert coat was short to just below hip length. The paletot was a semi-long to calf length lightweight summer coat and the Raglan overcoat by 1898 retained its deep-cut armholes.

Footwear Pointed boots and shoes were now very popular for men and spats in white or fawn were worn by all classes.

Headwear No fashion-conscious gentleman would venture out of doors without a hat. The top hat or silk hat retained its long popularity and was worn with the frock and morning coats and with evening dress. Bowlers were gaining in popularity and were known in the United States as a derbys. The soft felt 'wide awake' hat with a low crown, and the stiff felt Homburg hat with a groove from front to back, were both fashionable. The trilby which was similar to the Homburg but in a soft felt was not as popular at this time. Straw hats were worn mainly in the summertime or late spring. Caps, which were working class headgear were also worn by the fashionable wealthy classes — but only in the country.

Hairstyles The hair was now cut very short with a side parting and moustaches were worn by all classes.

Accessories As with the female fashion gloves were an essential part of the well-dressed gentleman's apparel. These were short in fawn or grey but always white for evening wear. Walking sticks or umbrellas were always carried, the sticks were of light cane but in 1897 malacca canes became more popular. Umbrellas were carried furled — that is, closed and tightly rolled.

Male stage costume of 1889

STAGE PROPERTIES

Naval officer 1841

American naval officer 1840

Apart from the actual stage set itself, everything within that set is a stage property. Curtains, furnishings, coverings, trinkets, ornaments, and hand-carried properties such as cigars, cigarettes, umbrellas, sticks, masks, swords, guns, musical instruments etc, all come under the heading of properties or 'props' as they are also known.

If the set-designer is not capable of making the various articles for the play then it is important to find someone who can. The ideal choice for a property master is a person who is skilful not only in the art of modelling and casting, reproducing in papier mâché or some other material, but also extremely clever with his hands generally. The strangest items for stage use are often requested and need a full-time miracle worker to produce them! As I have already stated in my introduction, never place stage properties low down in priority on the designer's working plan. A set without properties is just an empty shell with little or no life or atmosphere. No matter how well a set is designed, without properties it lacks lustre and authenticity.

Research for stage properties is similar to that undertaken by the costume designer and the search of museums, theatres, libraries, books etc, must be the foundation study towards the art of the set designer.

It is the set designer's job to select or design the properties, be they curtains, coverings or furnishings in the characteristic styles and patterns of the period. A word of warning however will not come amiss here: if a pattern is required, never choose from a small section of a pattern as this is most confusing and can lead to a great many faults and disappointments. A large piece of the pattern or the whole of the pattern (actual size) should be seen, whether purchased or painted, before any final decision. In the case of stage properties such as curtains and coverings careful study should be applied as to the type of stage lighting required

American soldier of 1862

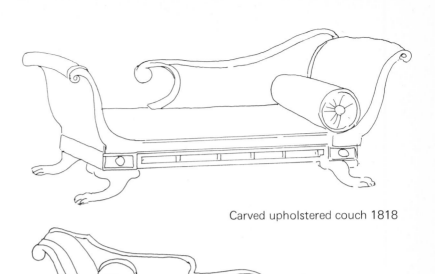

Carved upholstered couch 1818

United States cavalry, 1890

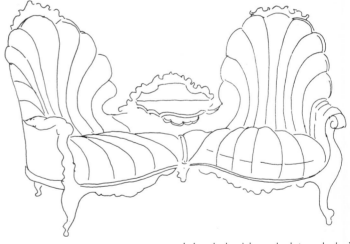

Upholstered sofa 1820

Joined double upholstered chair 1851

Russian helmet, 1856

as part of the overall planning of the stage set. Harmonious blending could be seriously affected by the choice of the wrong colouring effects under stage lighting. It is important to remember the importance of this theatre science and the part it plays in the presentation of a play.

British staff officer 1856

British Hussar officer 1856

German Pickelhaube helmet 1900

Furniture Regency furniture followed closely the classical antiquity styles. The early part of the century continued with designs from Egyptian, Greek and Roman sources. The best-known features were the use of brass and bronze gilt ornamentations which were used prolifically as corner and foot pieces, the latter in paw or claw style. Furniture at this time was well designed and gracefully proportioned with a high standard of craftmanship. It was, however, in a few decades to degenerate into a heavy pomposity and to be greatly affected by the industrialization of the new machine age.

The late eighteenth-century Empire neo-classicism style followed faithfully the rolled back Roman seats with the outward bowed legs and the Greek ceremonial throne styles which had carved arms and legs. These designs were now strengthened and made more comfortable with the seats and back supports often upholstered. The Regency trend was to

Victorian style papier mâché fourposter bed

Papier mâché chair 1820

Buttoned   upholstered   chair
1860

Regency chair 1820

make simpler forms of these Greek and Egyptian patterns and many of the ornate ornamentations were often modified to a simple turned or square block shape.

It is well for the set-designer and property master involved in an early nineteenth-century production to remember that the styles from the late eighteenth-century furniture still continued to be used and that a mixture of styles was very prevalent. The characteristic features were the massive supporting legs or pillars; these pillars were usually of human or animal carvings or some creative combination of both forms. Monoped supports decorated the lower parts of the furniture whilst eagle, lion or sphinx motifs were used for the ends of the chair arms. Small tables were replicas of the Greek tripods with tops of mahogany with brass or silver inlay or often with a marble slab supported on wooden legs. Both satin and rosewood were popular, but as the vogue was now to gild, paint or japan the wood, cheaper woods were used such as pine and deal; these woods were often used also for the carcase of the furniture as well as the veneered surfaces. Elm was more popular in the making of country-style furniture. Japanned furniture was used in the manufacture of bedroom furnishings often with gilt decoration. Brocades and silks were the usual covering for all upholstered furniture, although chintz and cotton were also used decorated with embroidery or printed birds, flowers or scenes of the period. The Regency period produced some new types of furnishings, especially in the field of well-designed bookcases, and it also saw the introduction of the upright pianoforte. Bedroom furniture changed little for an English setting, the fourposter bed remained supremely fashionable, whilst in a French setting the opposite was the case. The fourposter had long since gone out of fashion and a bed, not unlike a modern bed in use today, was now the accepted replacement. The Early Victorian period continued to make use of the Regency styles until around the middle of the century, when, with the appearance of great industrial wealth the demand for more items of furniture became the fashion. This increased demand for furniture had to be met by more mass-production by machinery, handmade furniture becoming almost a thing of the past.

The problem for the set designer when planning a set of this period is to create this feeling of a stage full of accessories. Whilst it is not a good practice to clutter the stage with unnecessary items, it is necessary, particularly in a Victorian

Victorian chair 1855

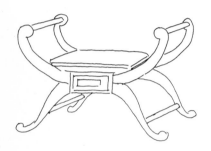

Stool with brass mountings 1820

Silver hand mirror 1860

setting, to show or to give the impression of less available floor space. Yet, for all practical purposes, the actors must be given adequate space for the stage action. There must also be, and this is a must for all interior sets, an atmospheric and realistic lived-in quality.

From this period the transition from the classical styles had now been completed, giving way to the Gothic heaviness and the ornate Rococo naturalistic carvings. Popular, although short-lived, were the papier mâché furniture and accessories, from tables and beds to trays and trinkets, usually japanned, sometimes inlaid with mother-of-pearl decoration. The whole atmosphere of this mid-Victorian era was one of being overcrowded; this was to continue almost throughout the rest of the century. For the set designer, the settings as far as stage properties are concerned should be that of many accessories and knick-knacks, stuffed birds, wax fruit, china figures and vases, glass ornaments, mirrors, antimacassars and all tables and chairs covered by lace and embroidered covers in wools and silks. Victorian factories began at this time to produce larger quantities of iron used in furniture; iron bedsteads now took the place of the wooden fourposter monstrosities, garden furniture and table legs were also popular in this material. The elegant line of the Grecian sofa was now replaced by the heavily carved and over-ornamented spiky horsehair variety.

From the middle of the century until the eighties, furniture remained very much the same, heavy, dull and ugly. From the eighties newer styles began to emerge and the heavy mahogany furniture began to be replaced by lighter styles in oak and walnut woods in imitation of Sheraton, Chippendale, Adam and the Jacobean fashions. By 1900 Art Nouveau had made its appearance. Plush, damask and leather upholstery was now becoming all the rage. Items of furniture in use throughout the nineteenth century are so numerous and diverse that the successful set designer must make a prolonged study of this aspect of stage properties for historical plays appropriate to this period.

As regards *musical instruments* the nineteenth century was known chiefly as an age of innovation and improvement and many of the instruments that are seen in the orchestras of today stem from this time. Woodwind instruments also achieved a great deal of improvement in their manufacture. The newer instruments were the piccolo, cor anglais, heckelphone and many others along with the upright piano. As many instruments as possible are illustrated.

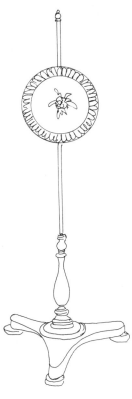

Victorian fire screen

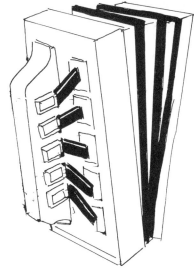

Accordion 1829

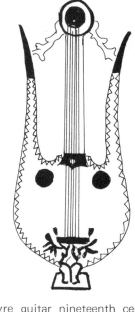

Lyre guitar nineteenth century

Gaslight pillar 1885

Spanish guitar nineteenth century

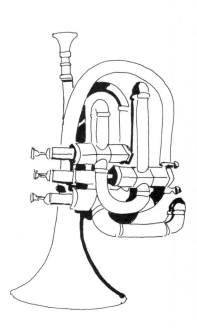

Nineteenth-century cornet

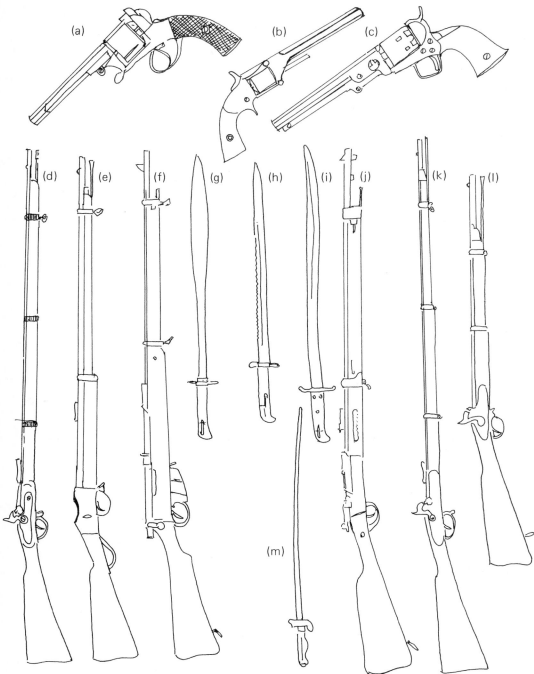

Weapons

a)   Bentley self-cocking pistol 1850
b)   Smith Wesson 1850
c)   Colt naval revolver 1851
d)   Snider-Enfield rifle 1867
e)   Martini Henri 1871
f)   Lee Enfield 1895
g)   Sword-type bayonet
h)   Sword-type bayonet
i)   Sword-type bayonet
j)   French Lebel rifle 1886-1893
k)   Long Enfield 1858
l)   Enfield artillery carbine 1858
m)   French bayonet

Scottish Claymore sword 1831

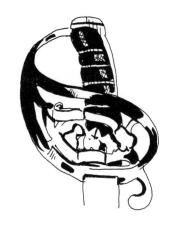

1870 pattern English sword

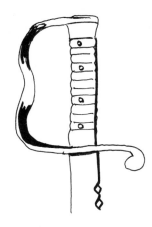

Hangar sword 1856

Artillery sword 1831

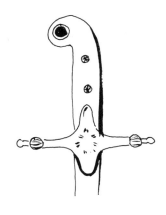

Scimitar sword 1831

Bandsman's sword 1895

◄ Sword crosspieces

1856 guard pattern ►

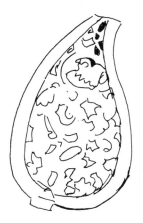

a)   Early nineteenth-century
French cuirassier
b)   Sword belt with sword and
bayonet

c)   Steel helmet with black
horsehair plume
d)   A cavalry pistol
e)   Pouch and carbine belt

f)   Two-piece cuirass
g)   Another type of cavalry
pistol
h)   Carbine musket

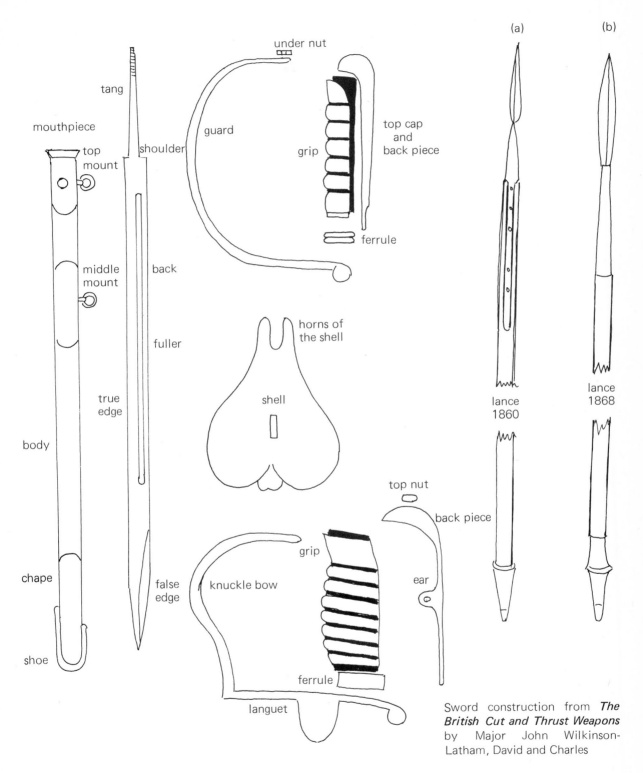

tang

mouthpiece

top
mount

shoulder

guard

under nut

grip

top cap
and
back piece

middle
mount

back

ferrule

fuller

horns of
the shell

true
edge

shell

body

top nut

back piece

chape

false
edge

knuckle bow

grip

ear

ferrule

shoe

languet

(a)

(b)

lance
1860

lance
1868

Sword construction from *The British Cut and Thrust Weapons* by Major John Wilkinson-Latham, David and Charles

83

Kitchen utensils Those utilized in the nineteenth century followed the styles established in the previous age, with the articles still being made from wood, brass, earthenware, pewter and iron. The difference was in their manufacture, as the mass-production methods were now in full operation.

Gas, and towards the end of the century, electricity, brought many improvements into use for domestic purposes and of course they were also used for theatre lighting. No upper-class stage set would be complete without Alexander Graham Bell's invention — the telephone. America was first in the field with this new instrument — Britain lagging showly behind, with the National Telephone Company (N.T.C.) not being formed until 1889. Coal was the usual heating system for nearly all buildings and open fireplaces and cooking ranges were the main source of energy for domestic heating and cooking. Coal-scuttles, fenders, pokers, tongs, firescreens were all very much a part of the interior scene. The development of motor cars or horseless carriages as they were known, also affected many aspects of life.

Weapons The machine age saw the development not only of clothes and furnishings but also of the weapons of war. Thus greater standardization and more conventional patterns were adopted by most countries. In the first part of the century the flintlock pattern was mainly used but by mid-century most guns were converted to the percussion system and adopted by all European countries as well as America. The periods of the Crimean War and the American Civil War saw great improvements and an increase in the numbers of weapons being manufactured. During the American Civil War the breech-loading rifle took over from the muzzle-loading rifle. By the end of the century cartridge breech-loaders, repeating rifles and many others came into fashion.

Iron coal scuttle 1880

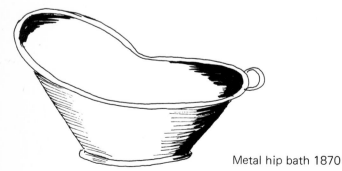

Metal hip bath 1870

84

STAGE SETTINGS

Many of the Victorian plays were interior sets. This rough layout is merely a guide for the young designer. On this plan should also be marked all furnishings and stage properties

Stage setting designing is in reality a combination of the arts of an architect and an interior designer. It is the designer who must supply the specialist knowledge, and transfer the ideas of the playwright and the producer into a practical set

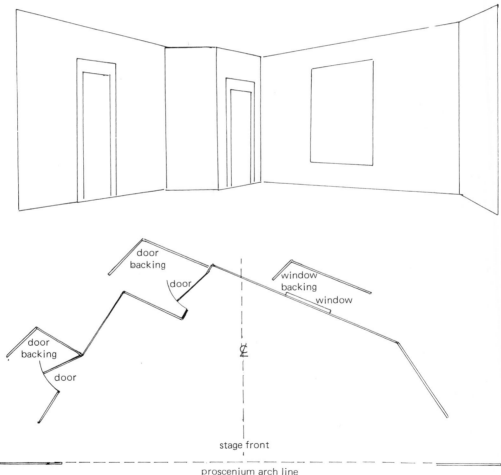

Exterior Set — simple rough sketch of scene, transformed into a practical stage setting

a) Background piece set against cyclorama

b) Groundrow piece — with this simple composition, great depth can be obtained for the scene

with all the mood and atmospheric conditions suitable for the play. It is for the set designer to work out and plan, through both reading and watching the play in rehearsals, the amount of space available for the building and layout of the scene. Every stage has a limited space and it is in the utilization of that space which is the set designer's creation.

Never plan or design a beautiful three-dimensional creation without first analysing the plot of the play. If he does not do this the designer may well see his dream setting gradually being torn apart by a somewhat vexed producer or actor who

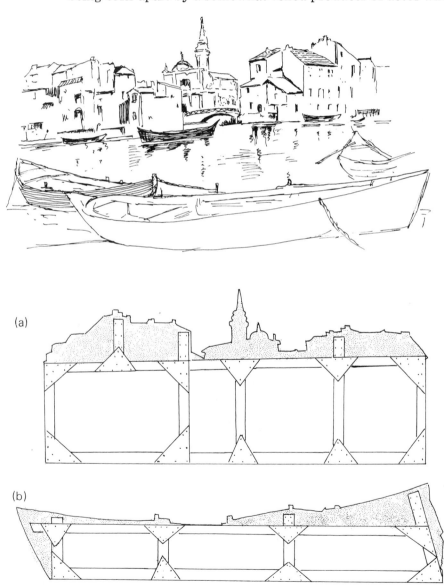

(a)

(b)

may be unable to move from A to B without great difficulty. The play is the most important thing and all else is subordinate to it, and the designer must realise from the outset that the set must conform to the requirements of the action of the play. Never underestimate the difficulties of stage set designing, this theatre art calls for a great deal of ability, dramatic imagination and above all a good comprehension of all the other theatre arts. A good designer is also one who will listen to the other professional theatre experts and co-ordinate the four basic arts of acting, lighting, scenery and costume.

The approach to outdoor settings and box, or interior, settings must be tackled separately. Whereas the interior set in its simplest form is built as a four-sided enclosure with the proscenium being the fourth wall, the question of masking does not occur to any great extent. An exterior setting is quite different and presents the stage set designer with exciting problems which in most cases probably prove more interesting than tackling a plain interior. Backcloths, groundrows and wings must be so designed and constructed not only to make the masking of the sides of the stage possible but also to mask, without hindering their important function, the top and side lighting. Further, to keep the set in the complete atmospheric mood, the borders (which help to mask the top lighting) must be incorporated into the set rather than being left as a border of plain gathered material.

Architecture   The study of the architecture and the interior designs of the nineteenth century does present many problems to the designer of stage settings. The playwrights of the period came from various countries and staged their plots within the confines of their own geographical territories. Therefore the set designer must be prepared for a prolonged study of various aspects of the different architecture of the countries around which the plot revolves. Such knowledge can only come from the research of the designers themselves and from the many sources which are available.

The nineteenth century perhaps more than any other century brought with it a variety of innovations and discoveries which surpassed all others in the way they changed people's daily lives.

Architecture and its position within the framework of the national life of the communities also presents a fascinating

a) Victorian latch window with half-draw curtains

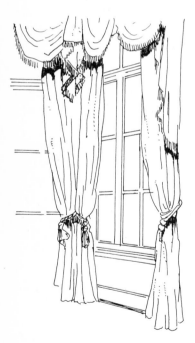

b) Large window with double draped curtains

study for the stage designer. Previously architecture was governed by climatic, geological, religious and historical considerations but with new discoveries most of these factors became less important. Steam transport alone lessened the importance of geology — for example to carry building materials from one brick-making country to a country where stone was predominant and *vice versa* without any great difficulty, was an important development. This situation does somewhat complicate the classification of architecture during that century, particularly during the latter years. Whereas in the past most architectural designs followed the traditional form of each country, in the nineteenth century with the added opportunities of faster and easier means of travel coupled with the invention of photography, more people were able to see and appreciate other countries' costume and architecture.

The early part of the nineteenth century saw the continuation of the graceful classical style of the last century, although this now faced strong competition from the Greek influence and the Romantic movement; classical design however never entirely lost its influence throughout the century. The desire for something new guided by such romantic writers as Sir Walter Scott found its channel in a return of the Gothic school of thought.

The competitive battle of the styles continued throughout the nineteenth century. With the growing influence of the wealthy middle classes, the building of large houses became very fashionable. These houses were built in a mass-produced style with the influences of gothic architecture and a variety of ornate decoration taken from mediaeval art. Victorian architecture at times reflected a haphazard adoption of almost every type of architecture from almost every country, much of it being a mixture of the wishes of the architect and the owner.

One of the greatest contributions to architecture during the nineteenth century was the application and development of iron and glass. It was the engineers who at that time gained the most dramatic success. The innovation of the railway brought with it the technical improvement of cast iron and this led to classical and gothic style structures being built in that material, such as railway stations, bridges and even park bandstands. Many of these still exist and can be seen in most large towns. The set designer could well afford a little study of these iron structures, to further his

c) Style of mahogany type baluster 1860-65

d) Styles of iron balusters popular in the Victorian period

insight of Victorian engineering architecture.

Country houses especially began to be built in neo-Jacobean style during the last decade of the century, although building generally became more traditional in construction with plain simple lines and the Rococo style ornamentation becoming unfashionable.

As many of the plays of the period made interiors the focal point it is important for the designer to study with great care the changes which took place over the century. During the early part of the century and the Regency period the classical influence still prevailed. The interiors usually had white plaster ceilings, cornice and frieze, the wallpapers being in delicate classical shades of pastel colouring. Woodwork was usually painted white and floors were of polished oak. The early Victorian interiors still maintained the white plaster ceilings, cornice and frieze with the white painted woodwork, but the wallpaper became less picturesque and used vertical line patterns more. From 1835 the colour schemes became darker and by mid-century the wallpapers were decorated with large floral motifs and the woodwork was painted in a dull heavy brown. The whole impression of the interiors was of sombre, dark, but rich colour schemes with complex chimney pieces of polished wood, fringed draperies and black polished iron fire grates.

The last decade of the century saw the interior, following the example of the exterior designs, beginning to be less cluttered with decoration, although the overcrowded rooms continued into the next century.

The set designer's problem in this era is not the lack of stage material but rather the abundance of properties which must be incorporated to give the polished, finished effect that is so important to the stage production as a whole.

Colours in stage setting designs as with the other arts of costume and properties, must be selected with great care and attention. The designing should be planned with stage lighting very much in mind, as all colours undergo a certain transformation under lighting conditions. A discussion with the lighting expert must be a top priority. A brief example is the use of blue; this is not an easy colour to light, since blues of the lightish tinge tend to change under the controversial red lighting to a dirty grey tone or to all shades of mauve. If in a darker blue it changes to shades of darkish grey or black. Red, a very powerful colour, should be used with caution.

STAGE LIGHTING

Stage lighting has developed over the years to become an integral part of stage presentation, an additional art to the other theatrical sciences. The nineteenth century saw the first real development of lighting for the stage with the introduction of gas stage-lighting. This was the first stage in the provision of a source of powerful illumination which could be controlled.

In the 1860s came the first focus lamp — the lime light. This was developed and improved and such was the effect of the improvements in stage illumination that with it came the opportunity to completely change the style of acting. But the invention of the electric lighting system in 1878 ultimately brought about, at the Savoy Theatre, London, in 1880, the first stage lighting equipment which laid the foundations for this new theatre art.

Today stage lighting is a necessity and must be treated with the same careful planning as all the other theatre arts. The stage designer must from the outset of the production have a clear idea when designing the set or sets as to their lighting plots. There is nothing worse than 'making do' by adding a light here and a light there after the set has been built. The set should be designed to accommodate any special lighting effects required. Terms of 'lighting thinking' must be taken into account early in the planning stage. For example, there should be sufficient illumination of the stage set to enable the audience to see all that the producer wishes them to see; there should be a flexible variation possible to allow for a change in mood or to focus and increase the audience's attention on some important plot activity. Set designing and illumination must be combined to help the atmospheric and emotional development of the play. The intelligent manipulation of lighting can transform a stage set into a world of realism or of symbolic fantasy.

The art of stage lighting is such that it offers the designers opportunities for individualism in conjunction with the scenic and costume effects. To change this medium into an expression of realism or symbolic atmosphere and to intensify the effects required, white light should be used sparingly and colour should be used in the same way as an artist uses his paints, blending and mixing until the correct effect has been achieved. It is a sobering thought for the designers of both stage sets and costume to realize that their well-designed sets and beautiful costumes could be utterly ruined by the misfortune of incorrect and unimaginative lighting. By studying lighting attentively they can transform its possible effects and help it bring life to their own efforts.

The vast subject of stage lighting is so interesting and intriguing and can be discussed at such length that this small volume is insufficient. The many facets of colour combinations and their effects both psychologically and symbolically are without parallel in the long history of the theatre. It is my hope that both the set designers and costume designers will include in their studies and in their designs this very important part of the theatre art.

Lighting equipment today is not cheap, but its importance is obvious and every effort should be made to at least obtain the minimum necessary for the stage production. There are many places that offer electrical equipment for weekly or daily hire. Depending on the number of performances to be given, the costs can be cut to a minimum. This also highlights the necessity of good sense in planning correctly by including the type and number of lights required for the set and the number of colours needed.

CHOOSING A PLAY

The art of choosing an historical play is not without its fair share of problems, especially when those of the nineteenth century are involved. Here is a period which combines all the creative arts of the theatre into masterpieces of ingenuity. It is supremely difficult for those who perform these historical plays to suggest to their audience the sombreness and heaviness of the Victorian age and still retain a degree of entertainment.

Again the choice is made that much easier by the amount of talent shown by those who wrote the plays of that age. It was indeed an era of theatrical and literary excellence, with such names as Charles Dickens, Ibsen, Chekhov, Robert Louis Stephenson, Drinkwater and many others.

For the more serious societies the choice is wide as to which dramatist is chosen to suit the type of play they would like to perform, as the nineteenth century produced every type of playwright. For the musical and lighter entertainment there is also an abundance of material from the operas, musical comedies and the very popular Music Hall. The latter group nowadays find a great many followers among the various choral societies which exist in every country.

The selected plays offered in my list are but a fraction of the plays available but as can be seen their writers comprise a wide range of nationalities. The ability and resourcefulness of all those concerned in the making of the play be they producer, costume or set designers, lighting or property master must govern the choice of play. All things are possible, but always remember that the choice of any play is controlled by all-important factors such as finance, the acting ability of the group, the time available for rehearsals and the extent of stage and equipment availability. The essential play-reading will ultimately decide to what extent the production team can take on both on the artistic and technical side.

Nearly all the plays in the list compiled, have, at some time or other, been performed by both professional and amateur stage societies, drama groups and schools.

Dramatizations of the following:
Oliver Twist, Nicholas Nickleby, David Copperfield, A Christmas Carol, Barnaby Rudge by Charles Dickens
Uncle Tom's Cabin and *The Little Minister* by J M Barrie
Cranford by Mrs Gaskell
East Lynn (melodrama) by Mrs Henry Wood

A selection of plays:
Milestones by Arnold Bennett and Edward Knoblock
The Professor's Love Story by J M Barrie
Peter Ibbetson by George du Maurier
The Streets of New York, London Assurance and *The Octoroon* by Dion Boucicault
Le Pére by Francois Coppée
The Three Daughters of M. Dupont by Brieux
Sherlock Holmes by Arthur Conan Doyle
Uncle Vanya, The Seagull, Three Sisters, The Bear and *The Proposal* by Anton Chekhov
La Dame aux Camelias by Alexandre Dumas
Abraham Lincoln by John Drinkwater
The Barretts of Wimpole Street by Rudolf Besier
Shore Acres by James G Herne
The League of Youth, Pillars of Society, The Doll's House, Ghosts, An Enemy of the People, Wild Duck, Rosmersholm, Hedda Gabler, The Master Builder and *Little Eyolf* by Henrik Ibsen
Fashion by Anna Cora Mowatt
Hazel Kirke by Steele Mackaye
Our American Cousin and *Ticket of Leave Man* by Tom Taylor
A Month in the Country by Ivan Turgeniev
Becky Sharpe by Langdon Mitchell
Trelawney of the Wells, The Second Mrs Tanqueray, The Magistrate, The Amazons, The Notorious Mrs Ebbsmith and *The Gay Lord Quex* by Arthur Wing Pinero
Society and *Caste* by Tom Robertson
The Power of Darkness, Resurrection and *Anna Karenina* (dramatization) by Tolstoy

Dr Jekyll and Mr Hyde by Robert Louis Stephenson

Mrs Warren's Profession, Arms and the Man, Candida and
    You Never Can Tell by George Bernard Shaw

Magda by Sudermann

The Affairs of Anatol by Schnitzler

*Lady Windermere's Fan, A Woman of No Importance, An
    Ideal Husband* and *The Importance of Being Earnest*
    by Oscar Wilde

Trial by Jury, HMS Pinafore, Pirates of Penzance and *Patience*
    by Gilbert and Sullivan

English Music Hall was established in 1843 and the hey-day
was between 1890-1912. Musical comedy flourished during
this period and many of the costumes shown in this volume
are like those worn in the different productions.

INDEX